Microsoft® Office
Excel® 2010

Level 2

Microsoft® Office Excel® 2010: Level 2

Part Number: 084577
Course Edition: 2.0

NOTICES

HELP US IMPROVE OUR COURSEWARE

Your comments are important to us. Please contact us at Element K Press LLC, 1-800-478-7788, 500 Canal View Boulevard, Rochester, NY 14623, Attention: Product Planning, or through our Web site at **http://support.elementkcourseware.com**.

Microsoft® Office Excel® 2010: Level 2

About This Course

In the first course, *Microsoft® Office Excel® 2010: Level 1,* you learned the basic skills needed to create and format spreadsheets, perform simple calculations, modify spreadsheet elements, and print workbooks. To increase your proficiency, you need to know how to perform advanced calculations, analyze and interpret data, and display spreadsheet data in a visually effective manner. In this course, you will use advanced formulas and tools to streamline and analyze spreadsheet data. You will also enhance the look and appeal of your workbooks by adding charts and other graphical objects.

Excel is a powerful data analysis application used for manipulating large amounts of numerical data. Knowing the advanced features of this software will aid you in processing complex data and enhancing spreadsheet reports and charts.

Course Description

Target Student

This course is meant for those desiring to gain advanced skill sets necessary for calculating data using functions and formulas, sorting and filtering data, using PivotTables and PivotCharts for analyzing data, and customizing workbooks.

Course Prerequisites

Before starting this course, students are recommended to take the following Element K course or have equivalent knowledge: *Microsoft® Office Excel® 2010: Level 1.*

Course Objectives

In this course, you will use advanced formulas and work with various tools to analyze data in spreadsheets. You will also organize table data, present data as charts, and enhance the look and appeal of workbooks by adding graphical objects.

You will:

- Use advanced formulas.
- Organize worksheet and table data using various techniques.
- Create and modify charts.
- Analyze data using PivotTables, Slicers, and PivotCharts.
- Insert and modify graphic objects in a worksheet.

- Customize and enhance workbooks and the Microsoft Office Excel environment.

How to Use This Book

As a Learning Guide

This book is divided into lessons and topics, covering a subject or a set of related subjects. In most cases, lessons are arranged in order of increasing proficiency.

The results-oriented topics include relevant and supporting information you need to master the content. Each topic has various types of activities designed to enable you to practice the guidelines and procedures as well as to solidify your understanding of the informational material presented in the course.

At the back of the book, you will find a glossary of the definitions of the terms and concepts used throughout the course. You will also find an index to assist in locating information within the instructional components of the book.

In the Classroom

This book is intended to enhance and support the in-class experience. Procedures and guidelines are presented in a concise fashion along with activities and discussions. Information is provided for reference and reflection in such a way as to facilitate understanding and practice.

Each lesson may also include a Lesson Lab or various types of simulated activities. You will find the files for the simulated activities along with the other course files on the enclosed CD-ROM. If your course manual did not come with a CD-ROM, please go to **http:// elementkcourseware.com** to download the files. If included, these interactive activities enable you to practice your skills in an immersive business environment, or to use hardware and software resources not available in the classroom. The course files that are available on the CD-ROM or by download may also contain sample files, support files, and additional reference materials for use both during and after the course.

As a Teaching Guide

Effective presentation of the information and skills contained in this book requires adequate preparation. As such, as an instructor, you should familiarize yourself with the content of the entire course, including its organization and approaches. You should review each of the student activities and exercises so you can facilitate them in the classroom.

Throughout the book, you may see Instructor Notes that provide suggestions, answers to problems, and supplemental information for you, the instructor. You may also see references to "Additional Instructor Notes" that contain expanded instructional information; these notes appear in a separate section at the back of the book. PowerPoint slides may be provided on the included course files, which are available on the enclosed CD-ROM or by download from **http://elementkcourseware.com**. The slides are also referred to in the text. If you plan to use the slides, it is recommended to display them during the corresponding content as indicated in the instructor notes in the margin.

The course files may also include assessments for the course, which can be administered diagnostically before the class, or as a review after the course is completed. These exam-type questions can be used to gauge the students' understanding and assimilation of course content.

As a Review Tool

Any method of instruction is only as effective as the time and effort you are willing to invest in it. In addition, some of the information that you learn in class may not be important to you immediately, but it may become important later on. For this reason, we encourage you to spend some time reviewing the topics and activities after the course.

As a Reference

The organization and layout of this book make it an easy-to-use resource for future reference. Taking advantage of the glossary, index, and table of contents, you can use this book as a first source of definitions, background information, and summaries.

Course Icons

Icon	Description
	A **Caution Note** makes students aware of potential negative consequences of an action, setting, or decision that are not easily known.
	Display Slide provides a prompt to the instructor to display a specific slide. Display Slides are included in the Instructor Guide only.
	An **Instructor Note** is a comment to the instructor regarding delivery, classroom strategy, classroom tools, exceptions, and other special considerations. Instructor Notes are included in the Instructor Guide only.
	Notes Page indicates a page that has been left intentionally blank for students to write on.
	A **Student Note** provides additional information, guidance, or hints about a topic or task.
	A **Version Note** indicates information necessary for a specific version of software.

Course Requirements

Hardware

For this course, you will need one computer for each student and the instructor. Each computer should have the following hardware configuration:

- A 1 GHz Pentium-class processor or faster.
- A minimum of 256 MB of RAM. (512 MB of RAM is recommended).
- A 10 GB hard disk or larger. You should have at least 1 GB of free hard disk space available for the Office installation.
- A CD-ROM drive.
- A keyboard and mouse or other pointing device.
- A 1024 x 768 resolution monitor is recommended.
- Network cards and cabling for local network access.
- Internet access (contact your local network administrator).
- A printer (optional) or an installed printer driver.

- A projection system to display the instructor's computer screen.

Software

- Microsoft® Office Professional Plus 2010 Edition
- Microsoft® Office Suite Service Pack 1
- Microsoft® Windows® XP Professional with Service Pack 2

This course was developed using the Windows XP operating system; however, the manufacturer's documentation states that it will also run on Windows Vista. If you use Vista, you might notice some slight differences when performing the activities.

Class Setup

Initial Class Setup

For initial class setup:

1. Install Windows XP Professional on an empty partition.

    ■ Leave the Administrator password blank.

    ■ For all other installation parameters, use values that are appropriate for your environment (see your local network administrator for details).

2. On Windows XP Professional, disable the **Welcome** screen. (This step ensures that students will be able to log on as the Administrator user regardless of what other user accounts exist on the computer.)

    a. Click **Start** and choose **Control Panel→User Accounts.**

    b. Click **Change The Way Users Log On And Off.**

    c. Uncheck **Use Welcome Screen.**

    d. Click **Apply Options.**

3. On Windows XP Professional, install Service Pack 2. Use the Service Pack installation defaults.

4. On the computer, install a printer driver (a physical print device is optional). Click **Start** and choose **Printers and Faxes.** Under **Printer Tasks,** click **Add a Printer** and follow the prompts.

    If you do not have a physical printer installed, right-click the printer and choose **Pause Printing** to prevent any print error message.

5. Run the **Internet Connection Wizard** to set up the Internet connection as appropriate for your environment if you did not do so during installation.

6. Display known file type extensions.

    a. Open **Windows Explorer** (right-click **Start** and then choose **Explore.**)

    b. Choose **Tools→Folder Options.**

    c. On the **View** tab, in the **Advanced Settings** list box, uncheck **Hide Extensions For Known File Types.**

    d. Click **Apply,** and then click **OK.**

    e. Close **Windows Explorer.**

7. Log on to the computer as the Administrator user if you have not already done so.

8. Perform a complete installation of Microsoft Office Professional 2010.

9. In the **User Name** dialog box, click **OK** to accept the default user name and initials.

10. In the **Microsoft Office 2010 Activation Wizard** dialog box, click **Next** to activate the Office 2010 application.

11. When the activation of Microsoft Office 2010 is complete, click **Close** to close the **Microsoft Office 2010 Activation Wizard** dialog box.

12. In the **User Name** dialog box, click **OK.**

13. In the **Welcome To Microsoft 2010!** dialog box, click **Finish.** You must have an active Internet connection in order to complete this step. Here, you have to select the **Download And Install Updates From Microsoft Update When Available (Recommended)** option so that whenever there is a new update it gets automatically installed on your system.

14. After the Microsoft Update is run, in the **Microsoft Office** dialog box, click **OK.**

15. On the course CD-ROM, open the 084577 folder. Then, open the Data folder. Run the 084577dd.exe self-extracting file located in it. This will install a folder named 084577Data on your C drive. This folder contains all the data files that you will use to complete this course. If your course did not come with a CD, please go to **http:// elementkcourseware.com** to download the data files.

   Within each lesson folder, you may find a Solution folder. This folder contains solution files for the lesson's activities and lesson lab, which can be used by students to check their end results.

16. If necessary, minimize the **Language** bar.

Customize the Windows Desktop

Customize the Windows desktop to display the **My Computer** and **My Network Places** icons.

1. On the desktop, right-click and choose **Properties.**

2. Select the **Desktop** tab.

3. Click **Customize Desktop.**

4. In the **Desktop Items** dialog box, check **My Computer** and **My Network Places.**

5. Click **OK** and click **Apply.**

6. Close the **Display Properties** dialog box.

Before Every Class

1. Log on to the computer as the Administrator user.

2. Delete any existing data file from the C:\084577Data folder.

3. Extract a fresh copy of the course data files from the CD-ROM provided with the course manual, or download the data files from **http://elementkcourseware.com**.

List of Additional Files

Printed with each activity is a list of files students open to complete that activity. Many activities also require additional files that students do not open, but are needed to support the file(s) students are working with. These supporting files are included with the student data files on the course CD-ROM or data disk. Do not delete these files.

1 | Calculating Data with Advanced Formulas

Lesson Time: 1 hour(s), 30 minutes

Lesson Objectives:

In this lesson, you will use advanced formulas.

You will:

- Apply cell and range names.
- Calculate data across worksheets.
- Use specialized functions.
- Analyze data with logical and lookup functions.

Introduction

As you continue working with Microsoft® Office Excel®, you have probably learned new skills and explored new functions, for example, to generate new data from an existing set of data using basic formulas in a worksheet. Performing sophisticated calculations in a worksheet or across multiple worksheets is the hallmark of a more advanced user of Excel. In this lesson, you will create advanced formulas in a workbook.

Ever tried figuring out how much you can afford to pay for a new house and what your loan payments will be, say, over a period of ten years? It can be a frustrating experience trying to determine each of your payments for the said period. Excel offers built-in functions for performing calculations in your workbook. All you need to do is input data and select a function to perform the calculation and display the result.

TOPIC A
Apply Cell and Range Names

In this lesson, you will calculate data using advanced formulas in your workbook. A straight-forward way of constructing complex formulas lies in using names instead of cell addresses to refer to cell ranges. In this topic, you will apply cell and range names.

The more complex a formula is, the harder it can be to determine exactly what data is used in which part of the formula. When you use a range name, you can easily determine which data range is referenced in the formula.

Range Names

A *range name* is a descriptive label assigned to one or more cells for referring to them in a formula. The cells may be located anywhere in a workbook; in case of multiple cell ranges, they may be adjacent or nonadjacent. When you select a range of cells that have been assigned a name, the range name is displayed in the Name box. A range name must start with a letter, cannot contain spaces, and can be up to 255 characters long. It is good practice to use range names that are short, easy to remember, and descriptive enough to allow you to identify their function.

Excel allows you to limit the scope of a range name to either a worksheet or workbook. If the scope is set for a worksheet, then the range name cannot be used to refer to more than one range in a worksheet. It can, however, be used on another worksheet. If the scope is set for a workbook, the range name cannot be reused anywhere on the workbook.

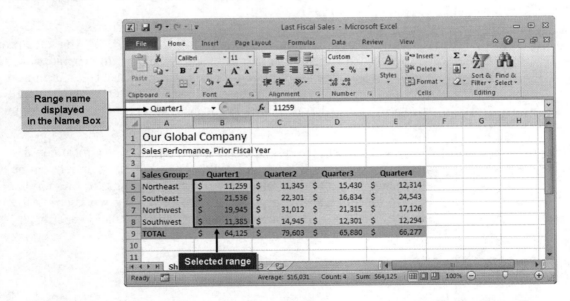

Figure 1-1: *When a named range is selected, the range name appears in the Name Box.*

Name Manager

Use the Name Manager to create, edit, or delete range names. The Name Manager provides a complete list of range names in a workbook.

How to Apply Cell and Range Names

Procedure Reference: Name a Cell Range from the Name Box

To name a cell range from the Name box and verify the result:

1. Select the range you want to name.
2. To the left of the formula bar, click in the **Name** box, type a range name of your choice, and press **Enter.**
3. Verify that the range is correctly named.
   a. Click any cell outside the selected range.
   b. Click the **Name** box drop-down menu and choose the range name.

Procedure Reference: Name a Cell Range with the New Name Dialog Box

To name a cell range with the New Name dialog box:

1. Select the range to be named.
2. Open the **New Name** dialog box.
   - On the **Formulas** tab, in the **Defined Names** group, from the **Define Name** drop-down menu, choose **Define Name.**
   - Or, in the **Defined Names** group, click **Name Manager** and then click **New.**
3. In the **New Name** dialog box, in the **Name** text box, enter the range name of your choice.
4. If necessary, using the **Scope** drop-down list, define the range name's scope.
   - Select **Workbook** to declare the scope throughout the entire workbook.
   - Or, select a worksheet name to declare the scope for a particular worksheet.

 By declaring the scope for a specific worksheet, it is possible to use the same name multiple times in a workbook.

5. If desired, type comments to describe the range name.
6. In the **Refers To** text box, select what the range refers to.
   - A cell reference, that is, one cell or a group of cells.
   - A constant: (=[*number or text*]).
   - Or, a formula: (=[*formula*]).
7. Click **OK.**
8. If necessary, close the **Name Manager** dialog box.

Procedure Reference: Name Cell Ranges Using Worksheet Data

To use worksheet data to create range names:

1. Select the range.
2. On the **Formulas** tab, in the **Defined Names** group, click **Create from Selection.**
3. In the **Create Names from Selection** dialog box, in the **Create names from values in the** section, check the desired check boxes to use the contents of the top or bottom row or the right or left column as range names.
4. Click **OK.**

Procedure Reference: Edit a Named Range

To edit a named range:

1.   Select the named range to verify that it is the range whose name you want to change.

2.   On the **Formulas** tab, in the **Defined Names** group, click **Name Manager.**

3.   In the **Name Manager** dialog box, from the list of named ranges, select the range name that you want to change and click **Edit.**

4.   In the **Edit Name** dialog box, type the new range name and add any new comments, if necessary.

5.   To change the cell references for the range, type the new references in the **Refers To** text box, or select the text box and then select the new range on the worksheet and click **OK.**

     For example, you might need to edit the cell references for the range if you have inserted a row or column that runs through the range.

6.   Click **Close** to close the **Name Manager** dialog box.

7.   Select the range name from the **Name** box drop-down list to verify the new name and cell range.

Procedure Reference: Delete a Range Name

To delete a range name:

1.   On the **Formulas** tab, in the **Defined Names** group, click **Name Manager.**

2.   In the **Name Manager** dialog box, select the range name or names that you want to delete.

     You can use **Shift + Click** or **Ctrl + Click** to select multiple names.

3.   Click **Delete** or press **Delete** on the keyboard and click **OK.**

4.   Close the **Name Manager** dialog box.

Procedure Reference: Include Range Names in Formulas

To include range names in formulas:

1.   Select the cell where you want to enter the formula.

2.   Start entering the formula in the formula bar or in the selected cell.

3.   At the point in the formula where you need to insert a cell or range address, insert the range name.

     ●   Type the range name, or type multiple range names, separated by commas.

     ●   Or, in the **Defined Names** group, click **Use In Formula** and select the range name from the drop-down list.

4.   Complete the entry of the formula.

 Range names refer to absolute cell addresses. When formulas that include range names are copied, they do not copy relative to their new location.

ACTIVITY 1-1
Managing Range Names in Workbooks

Data Files:

Last Fiscal Sales.xlsx

Scenario:

You are working in the sales department of Our Global Company (OGC) Bookstores. The company's board has asked you to submit a report on the total and average sales in different regions in different quarters for the last fiscal year. You entered the data in an Excel sheet and now want to apply range names for cell ranges so that it is easier to refer to them in the formulas.

1. Name the range B5:B8 as Quarter1.

   a. From the C:\084577Data\Calculating Data with Advanced Formulas folder, open the **Last Fiscal Sales.xlsx** file.

   b. Select the range **B5:B8.**

   c. To the left of the **Formula Bar**, click inside the **Name Box.**

   d. In the **Name Box**, enter the name of the range as *Quarter1*

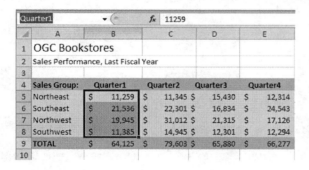

2. Verify that the range name is correctly applied.

   a. Deselect the range **B5:B8** by selecting any cell on the worksheet outside the range **B5:B8.**

   b. Select the range **B5:B8.**

    c.   In **Name Box**, observe that the name of the range is displayed as **Quarter1**.

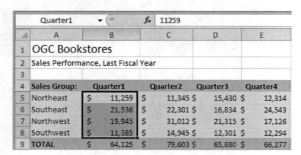

3.   Create named ranges for Quarter2 through Quarter4 using labels from the worksheet, and then create named ranges for the sales group regions.

    a.   Select the range **C4:E8.**

    b.   On the **Formulas** tab, in the **Defined Names** group, click **Create from Selection.**

    c.   In the **Create Names from Selection** dialog box, verify that **Top row** is checked by default and click **OK** to create the range name from the cell in the top row.

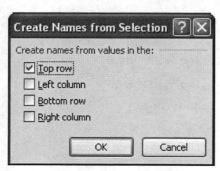

    d.   From the **Name Box** drop-down list, select **Quarter2.**

    e.   Observe that the range **C5:C8** is selected. Select the range **A5:E5.**

    f.   On the **Formulas** tab, in the **Defined Names** group, click **Create from Selection.**

    g.   In the **Create Names from Selection** dialog box, verify that **Left column** is checked and click **OK.**

    h.   From the **Name Box** drop-down list, select **Northeast** and observe that the range **B5:E5** is selected.

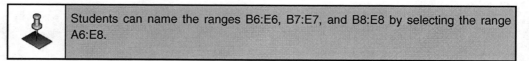

Students can name the ranges B6:E6, B7:E7, and B8:E8 by selecting the range A6:E8.

    i.   Repeat the steps from selecting the ranges through using the **Create Names from Selection** dialog box to name the ranges **B6:E6**, **B7:E7**, and **B8:E8** as Southeast, Northwest, and Southwest, respectively.

    j.   Select the range **B5:E6.**

    k.   To the left of the formula bar, click inside the **Name Box.**

l.   In the **Name Box**, enter the name of the range as *East*

m.   Similarly, name the range **B7:E8** as *West*

4.   Use Name Manager to rename the sales groups.

a.   On the **Formulas** tab, in the **Defined Names** group, click **Name Manager.**

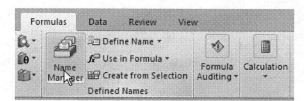

b.   In the **Name Manager** dialog box, select **Northeast** and click **Edit.**

c.   In the **Edit Name** dialog box, in the **Name** text box, type *NE* and click **OK.**

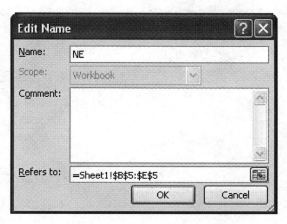

d.   Similarly, rename **Northwest, Southeast, and Southwest** to *NW, SE,* and *SW*, respectively.

e.   Close the **Name Manager** dialog box.

f.   In the **Name Box** drop-down, observe the modified names.

5.   Calculate the total and average sales for the East Coast and the West Coast.

a.   Select cell **B13.**

b.   In the **Function Library** group, click **AutoSum** and then click **Insert Function.**

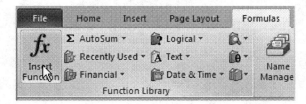

c.   In the **Functions Arguments** dialog box, in the **Number1** text box, type *NE*

d.   In the **Number2** text box, type *SE* and click **OK** to view the total sales in the East Coast region.

e. Similarly, enter the formula in cell **B14** to calculate the total sales for the West Coast region.

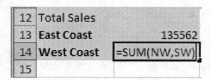

f. Select cell **B17**, click the **Autosum** drop-down and select **Average.**

g. Click **Insert Function**, and in the **Function Arguments** dialog box, in the **Number1** text box, type *East* and click **OK.**

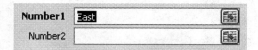

h. Similarly, in cell **B18**, enter the formula for calculating the average sales for the west region for the last fiscal.

i. Save the file as *My Last Fiscal Sales* and close it.

TOPIC B
Calculate Data Across Worksheets

In the previous topic, you made complex formulas simpler to read by using range names. Another way you can increase the complexity of your formulas is by using formulas that pull data from several worksheets. In this topic, you will calculate data across worksheets.

You may find that you have data located in several worksheets. You could cut and paste the data into a single worksheet for calculation purposes, but then you run the risk of original data changing. Instead, you can make your calculation span worksheets and not be restricted to one. This way your calculation will be accurate, regardless of where the data is found.

Three-Dimensional Cell References

Definition:

A *three-dimensional (3-D) cell reference* is a cell reference located in the same place on multiple worksheets. It can be used only in a workbook with multiple worksheets. Each 3-D reference contains a start point (the first worksheet), an end point (the last worksheet), and a cell reference. 3-D references can be used in some functions and certain formulas.

Example:

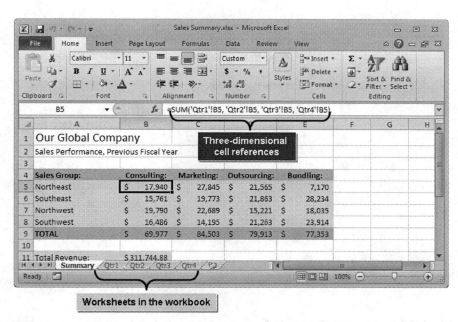

Figure 1-2: *Cells located on multiple worksheets can be referred using three-dimensional references.*

How to Calculate Data Across Worksheets

Procedure Reference: Enter Cells and Ranges from Multiple Worksheets into a Formula

To enter cells and ranges from multiple worksheets into a formula:

1. Select the cell where you want to enter the formula.

2. Start entering the formula in the formula bar or directly in the selected cell.

3. At the point in the formula where you need to insert a cell or range address, insert the appropriate multiple-sheet reference.

    ●   To refer to cells from a different worksheet, select the worksheet and then select the cell or range, or type the cell or range reference including the worksheet prefix.

    ●   Or, to insert a three-dimensional cell reference, select the first tab, Shift-click the tab for the last worksheet, and then select the cell or range on the first worksheet.

4. Complete entering the formula.

ACTIVITY 1-2
Creating Formulas Across Multiple Worksheets

Data Files:

Department Wise Revenue.xlsx

Scenario:

Your manager has asked you to create a summary page for a workbook that contains quarterly sales results for the last fiscal for different departments. After inserting the summary as the first page, you are about to enter the formulas on the Summary sheet. The formulas will refer to data from multiple worksheets.

1.   Calculate the Northeast sales team's contribution to consulting for the entire fiscal.

   a.   From the C:\084577Data\Calculating Data with Advanced Formulas folder, open the Department Wise Revenue.xlsx file.

   b.   On the **Summary** worksheet, select cell **B5**.

   c.   Type *=SUM(Qtr1!B5, Qtr2!B5, Qtr3!B5, Qtr4!B5)* and press **Enter.**

   d.   Observe that the formula you entered calculates the Northeast sales team's contribution to consulting for the entire fiscal.

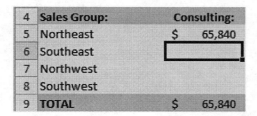

2.   Calculate the marketing sales for the entire fiscal for Northeast sales group.

   a.   Select cell **C5** and then type *=SUM(*

   b.   Select the **Qtr1** worksheet.

   c.   Hold down **Shift** and select the **Qtr4** worksheet.

   d.   In the **Qtr1** worksheet, select cell **C5** and then press **Enter.**

   e.   In the **Summary** worksheet, observe that the formula you entered calculated the marketing sales for the entire fiscal for Northeast sales group.

3.   Fill in the formulas for the rest of the Summary worksheet.

   a.   Select cell **C5.**

   b.   Copy the formula in cell **C5** to cells **D5** and **E5** using the fill handle.

   c.   Select the range **B5:E5.**

d. Drag the fill handle to **E8.**

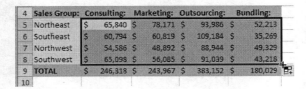

4	Sales Group:	Consulting:	Marketing:	Outsourcing:	Bundling:
5	Northeast	$ 65,840	$ 78,171	$ 93,986	$ 52,213
6	Southeast	$ 60,794	$ 60,819	$ 109,184	$ 35,269
7	Northwest	$ 54,586	$ 48,892	$ 88,944	$ 49,329
8	Southwest	$ 65,098	$ 56,085	$ 91,039	$ 43,218
9	**TOTAL**	$ 246,318	$ 243,967	$ 383,152	$ 180,029
10					

e. Save the file as ***My Department Wise Revenue*** and close it.

TOPIC C

Use Specialized Functions

In the previous topic, you used formulas that included numeric references from many different worksheets. You can also make formulas more complex by using functions that enable you to perform specialized operations, such as those that use non-numeric data. In this topic, you will use specialized functions to perform a variety of worksheet operations.

At times, you will need to use specialized functions to perform advanced calculations. Using specialized categories of functions will allow you to go beyond basic mathematics and perform operations on specialized types of data such as text, dates, and times.

Function Categories

Excel has 13 categories of functions, each with a specific use.

Category	Purpose
Financial	Functions that perform common accounting and financial calculations. The calculations are primarily based on depreciation of assets, investments, and loans. Each of these categories relies on data such as the interest rate, length of time, value of an item, and payment amount.
Date & Time	Functions that assign a serial number to date and time data in order to use the data in a calculation. Although the data is converted to a serial number, it is displayed in the worksheet as text. Date & Time functions range from a function that enters the current date into a worksheet such as **=TODAY()** or **=NOW()**, to functions that will calculate how much time has elapsed between a start time and an end time.
Math and trigonometric	Functions that are used to perform common mathematical and trigonometric calculations such as sine values, cosine values, tangent values, logarithms, and exponents.
Statistical	Functions that perform statistical analysis on a range of data in a worksheet or in a chart. The **AVERAGE** function is a simple example of a Statistical function that calculates the average of all the values in a range.
Lookup and reference	Functions that are used for finding values in a corresponding table or list and incorporating the data into the calculation. The two most popular lookup functions are **VLOOKUP** and **HLOOKUP.**
Database	Functions that perform database related operations on data that meets some criteria such as extracting a record based on a criterion.
Text	Functions that manipulate text in a worksheet. For example, to change the case of text, use the **UPPER, LOWER,** or **PROPER** function. To perform a find and replace in a formula, use **SUBSTITUTE** function and to extract a given number of characters a string, use the **LEFT** or **RIGHT** functions to extract the characters from left or right. The **LEN** function determines the number of characters in the cell. To concatenate two or more strings of text, you can use the **CONCATENATE** function by including the strings to be concatenated as arguments.
Logical	Functions that perform what-if analysis to see if a condition is true or false.

Category	Purpose
Information	Functions that perform analysis on a range of data to determine the type of data or formatting present in a cell. For example, you can use these functions to determine whether cells are blank or have data in them, or if a cell contains a formula with an error.
Engineering	Functions that perform various types of engineering conversions and tests.
Cube	Functions that are used to fetch data from Online Analytical Processing (OLAP) cubes. OLAP is a database technology used to make business-intelligence queries. For more information on OLAP support in Excel, see Excel Help.
Compatibility	Some functions in Excel have been replaced with new functions so as to improve their accuracy. The older versions of these functions are compatible with the previous versions and can be used in the place of new functions for performing the same operation. However, these functions may not be available in future versions of Excel.
User defined	These functions are not available in the Excel function library at the time of purchase and are taken from the add-ins that users install on their computers.

Function Syntax

Definition:

The *function syntax* refers to the structure and order of arguments in a function. The syntax displays the names of arguments, their order, and whether they are required or not. The syntax varies from function to function.

Example:

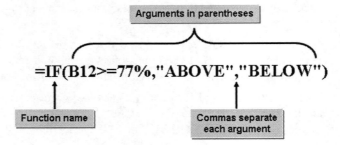

Figure 1-3: *The syntax of a function defines its structure.*

Function Entry Dialog Boxes

Excel provides two dialog boxes to guide you through selecting a function and its arguments.

Dialog Box Name	Description
Insert Function	Enables you to select the function from a list, grouped by category. There is descriptive text about the purpose of each function. This dialog box can help you locate the correct function as well as ensure that you spell the function properly.
Function Arguments	After you insert a function, you can use the **Function Arguments** dialog box to guide you through entering the arguments and data that follow the correct syntax for a specific function. There is descriptive text for each function argument as well as a link to context-sensitive help about the function.

 In previous versions of Excel, these two dialog boxes were grouped together as the **Function Wizard**. You might still see them referred to as the **Function Wizard** in some documentation.

Improvements to Excel Functions

Functions in Excel 2010 have undergone some changes and improvements. For instance:

- Algorithms of some formulas have been modified to provide more accurate results.
- Some functions have been renamed to make them more relevant to their operation.
- New functions have been added to the function library based on the best practices followed by users for computing data.
- And, users can use some functions with their older names, to provide backward compatibility with the previous version.

How to Use Specialized Functions

Procedure Reference: Insert Functions and Function Arguments Manually

To insert functions and function arguments in a worksheet manually:

1. Select the cell into which the formula will be placed.

2. Type the function and its arguments in the formula bar or directly in the selected cell. Press **Enter.**

Procedure Reference: Insert a Function with Function Entry Dialog Boxes

To insert a function with the **Insert Function** and **Function Arguments** dialog boxes:

1. Insert the function and open the **Function Arguments** dialog box.

   - Type the = sign in the formula bar or directly in the selected cell, followed by the name of the function and an open parenthesis, and then click **Insert Function** on the formula bar or in the **Function Library** group on the **Formulas** tab.

   - Or, click the drop-down list for the function category in the **Function Library** group, and select the function from the list.

   - Or, insert the function with the **Insert Function** dialog box.

     a. Click **Insert Function** on the formula bar or in the **Function Library** group.

     b. If necessary, from the **Or Select A Category** drop-down list, select the appropriate function category.

     c. In the **Select A Function** list box, either double-click the appropriate function, or select it and then click **OK.**

2. In the **Function Arguments** dialog box for the inserted function, enter the function arguments and then click OK.

ACTIVITY 1-3
Using Text Functions to Generate Reports

Data Files:

Employee List.xlsx

Scenario:

Your company has decided to provide each employee with a user ID that would be used in the employee's official Email address. The company has approved a standard for determining the user ID from the employee's first and last names. The IT services team has asked you to provide a detailed report containing details of employees in a specific format for use in official mail. You begin to create a report for the IT services team.

Also, your company has decided to award employees who have put in ten or more years of service with the company on the annual day and you need to identify those employees. As you are already creating a report, you decide to use the same worksheet to identify employees who have served the company for ten or more years and take a print out.

1. Enter the formulas to copy the employee IDs from Sheet1 to the Requirement worksheet.

   a. From the C:\084577Data\Calculating Data with Advanced Formulas folder, open the Employee List.xlsx file.

   b. On the **Sheet1** worksheet, observe the data in cell **A2.**

   c. On the **Requirement** worksheet, in cell **A2**, enter *=Sheet1!A2* to copy the data from cell **A2** of **Sheet1.**

   d. Observe that the data in the cell **A2** of **Sheet1** is copied to cell **A2** of the **Requirement** sheet.

   e. Copy the formula to the range **A3:A26.**

   f. Display the **Sheet1** worksheet.

2. Enter the formulas to generate data for the Full Name, User ID, and Department columns from the appropriate fields in Sheet1.

   a. On the **Sheet1** worksheet, observe the data in cells **B2, C2, E2,** and **F2** and display the **Requirement** worksheet.

   b. Scroll up, in cell **B2**, enter *=PROPER(CONCATENATE(Sheet1!B2,",",Sheet1!C2))* to concatenate the data in cells **B2** and **C2** of **Sheet1.**

   c. Observe that the data in the cells **B2** and **C2** of **Sheet1** is concatenated and converted to proper case and the result is displayed in cell **B2** of the **Requirement** sheet.

   d. Copy the formula to the range **B3:B26.**

   e. Scroll up, in cell **C2**, enter
=CONCATENATE(LEFT(Sheet1!C2,1),PROPER(Sheet1!B2)) to generate the user ID for the employees by concatenating the data in cells **B2** and **C2** of **Sheet1**, filtering unwanted characters from the last name.

   f. Observe that the formula displays the user ID for the first employee in cell **C2.**

   g. Copy the formula to the range **C3:C26.**

   h. Scroll up, in cell **D2**, enter **=CONCATENATE(Sheet1!F2," ",Sheet1!E2)** to concatenate the department ID and department name of the employees.

   i. Observe that the formula concatenates the department ID and department name of the first employee and displays them in cell **D2.**

   j. Copy the formula to the range **D3:D26.**

Full Name	User ID	Department
Comuntzis Mark	MComuntzis	121 Accounts and Finance
Filosa Alexandra	AFilosa	129 Tech.Support
Binga Mary	MBinga	111 Sales
Donnell Susan	SDonnell	130 Application Development
Carol Elizabeth	ECarol	130 Application Development
Decker Erica	EDecker	111 Sales
Clarke Joe	JClarke	130 Application Development
Chaffee Adam	AChaffee	130 Application Development
Desiato Barbara	BDesiato	130 Application Development
Chase Fred	FChase	122 Human Resources
Fern Elizabeth	EFern	121 Accounts and Finance
Cole Daniel	DCole	130 Application Development
Chu Laurie	LChu	111 Sales
Clark Drew	DClark	111 Sales
Ellis Janet	JEllis	129 Tech.Support
Chung Bob	BChung	122 Human Resources
Boller Mary	MBoller	121 Accounts and Finance
Ferris Jim	JFerris	121 Accounts and Finance
Clark John	JClark	122 Human Resources
Barry Angela	ABarry	111 Sales
Flanders Sabrina	SFlanders	111 Sales
Garwood Edward	EGarwood	130 Application Development
Howard Russel	RHoward	111 Sales
Wentworth Carl	CWentworth	129 Tech.Support
Blackwell John	JBlackwell	130 Application Development

   k. Display the **Sheet1** worksheet.

---

3. Enter the formulas to extract data for the Location and Extension fields from column G of Sheet1.

   a. On the **Sheet1** worksheet, observe the data in cell **G2** and display the **Requirement** worksheet.

   b. Scroll up, in cell **E2**, enter **=LEFT(Sheet1!G2,FIND("-",Sheet1!G2)-1)** to extract the characters on the left of the **-** symbol in the cell **G2** of **Sheet1** as the location name.

   c. Observe that the formula extracts the characters on the left of the **-** symbol for the data in cell **G2** of **Sheet1.**

   d. Copy the formula to the range **E3:E26.**

   e. Scroll up to cell **F2**, enter **=RIGHT(Sheet1!G2,4)** to extract the four rightmost characters from cell **G2** of **Sheet1.**

   f. Observe that the formula extracts and displays the four rightmost characters for the data in cell **G2** of **Sheet1.**

g.   Copy the formula to the range **F3:F26.**

Location	Extention
HQ	2146
Central	2946
HQ	2055
Central	2366
Central	2389
HQ	2099
Central	2309
Central	2301
Central	2326
HQ	2278
HQ	2151
Central	2354
HQ	2046
HQ	2054
Central	2965
HQ	2267
HQ	2178
HQ	2188
HQ	2200
HQ	2077
HQ	2096
Central	2362
HQ	2067
Central	2961
Central	2395

4.   Enter the formula that will add an * symbol to all the employees who have served in the company for ten years or more.

a.   Scroll up and to the right, in cell **G2**, enter *=IF(((TODAY()-Sheet1!D2)/365)>=10,"*","")* to add an asterisk symbol in the cell if the employee has served in the company for more than 10 years.

b.   Observe that an * symbol is displayed for the first employee.

c.   Copy the formula to the range **G3:G26.**

d.   Save the file as ***My Employee List*** and close it.

TOPIC D

Analyze Data with Logical and Lookup Functions

In the previous topic, you used a number of specialized formulas to perform a variety of advanced calculations. Two of the function categories, Logical and Lookup & Reference functions, are even more specialized and complex than the ones you have used so far. In this topic, you will analyze data with Logical and Lookup & Reference functions.

How many times have you been told the price of a product by a sales attendant, only to have it ring up differently at the billing counter? This kind of problem happens when out-of-date data is retrieved accidentally. When you use the Lookup & Reference function, you can be sure that you are always retrieving the most accurate data directly from the source. Each time the data is requested, you will be pulling the most current information available.

Logical Functions

Excel includes seven logical functions: AND, FALSE, IF, IFERROR, NOT, OR, and TRUE. Each function analyzes the contents of a cell and then returns a Boolean value, depending upon whether the cell contents match the function requirements.

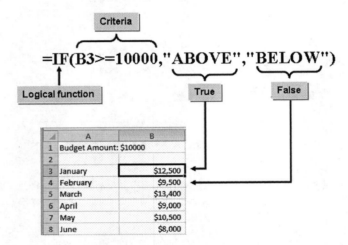

Figure 1-4: A function containing a logical operator.

The IF Function and Its Arguments

The IF function is used to evaluate a logical comparison, which is either true or false, and then take one of two possible actions based on the result. The function has three arguments:

- Logical_test
- Value_if_true
- Value_if_false

The function's syntax is: IF(logical_test, value_if_true, value_if_false)

The following table describes the arguments and their purpose.

Argument	Purpose
Logical_test	A comparison, such as E4>D4, which means "Is the number in cell E4 larger than the number in cell D4?" which is determined to be either true (yes) or false (no).
Value_if_true	The function's result will be displayed if the condition is true.
Value_if_false	The function's result will be displayed if the condition is false.

Functions Similar to the IF Function

There are several other useful functions that can perform calculations based on logical comparisons:

- SUMIF, which sums the data if it meets a criterion, and SUMIFS, which sums the data if it meets multiple criteria.

- COUNTIF, which counts the data if it meets a criterion, and COUNTIFS, which counts the data if it meets multiple criteria.

- AVERAGEIF, which averages the data if it meets a criterion, and AVERAGEIFS, which averages the data if it meets multiple criteria.

The syntax for SUMIF and AVERAGEIF is similar. It is: `FUNCTION NAME(range, criteria, sum_or_average range)`. If the argument sum_or_average range is omitted, the first argument, range is summed or averaged.

The syntax for COUNTIF is: `COUNTIF(range, criteria)`

The syntax for SUMIFS, COUNTIFS, and AVERAGEIFS is: `FUNCTION NAME(sum_or_average range, criteria range 1, criteria1, criteria range 2, criteria2)`

The AND Function and Its Arguments

The AND function is a Logical function used to evaluate two or more comparisons to determine whether they are all true. If any comparison within the AND function is determined to be false, the AND function returns a value of FALSE. If all the comparisons are true, the function returns a value of TRUE.

The AND function's syntax is: `AND(logical1, logical2, etc....)`

The following example is an instance of the AND function in which four criteria are evaluated:

    AND(E4>F9,D7<A5,M3<>T1,A1="FY 2010")

The OR Function and Its Arguments

The OR function is a Logical function used to evaluate two or more comparisons to determine whether any are true. If any comparison within the OR function is determined to be true, the OR function returns a value of TRUE. If none of the comparisons are true, the function returns a value of FALSE.

The OR function's syntax is: `OR(logical1, logical2, etc....)`

The following example is an instance of the OR function in which four criteria are evaluated:

    OR(E4>F9,D7<A5,M3<>T1,A1="FY 2010")

The NOT Function and Its Arguments

The NOT function is a Logical function used to return the opposite value than that determined by a logical comparison. If the comparison within the NOT function is determined to be true, the NOT function returns a value of FALSE. If the comparison is determined to be false, the function returns a value of TRUE.

The NOT function's syntax is: NOT(logical)

The following examples are instances in which the NOT function is evaluated to TRUE or FALSE:

- `NOT(27>3) evaluates to FALSE`
- `NOT(27<3) evaluates to TRUE`

Because 27>3 is a true statement, the function takes the opposite of true and returns a FALSE value. Because 27<3 is a false statement, the function takes the opposite of false and returns TRUE.

The IFERROR Function and Its Arguments

The IFERROR function is a Logical function that handles errors encountered by expressions contained within them. If the interior expression within the IFERROR function has no error, the IFERROR function returns the value of the interior expression. If the interior expression returns an error, the IFERROR function returns a text or numeric value.

The IFERROR function's syntax is: IFERROR(value, value_if_error)

The following expression would return a numeric value if cell C2 contained a number other than zero:

```
IFERROR(B4/C2,"Can't be computed.")
```

The following expression would return the message "Can't be computed" if cell C2 contained a zero or no value, which would cause a division-by-zero error:

```
IFERROR(B4/C2,"Can't be computed")
```

How the Lookup and Reference Functions Work

There are a number of Lookup & Reference functions that use the selected data in the current worksheet to locate similar data in other worksheets. The identified data can be displayed in a cell or used in a calculation. Data used in a Lookup & Reference function can be in the same workbook or another. Lookup & Reference functions are primarily used as part of a formula and not by themselves.

VLOOKUP and HLOOKUP Functions

The *VLOOKUP* function is one of the most popular lookup functions that searches vertically across a range's row headings and retrieves the information from the row that contains the value being searched. The *HLOOKUP* function searches horizontally across a table's column headings to locate and retrieve the information from the column.

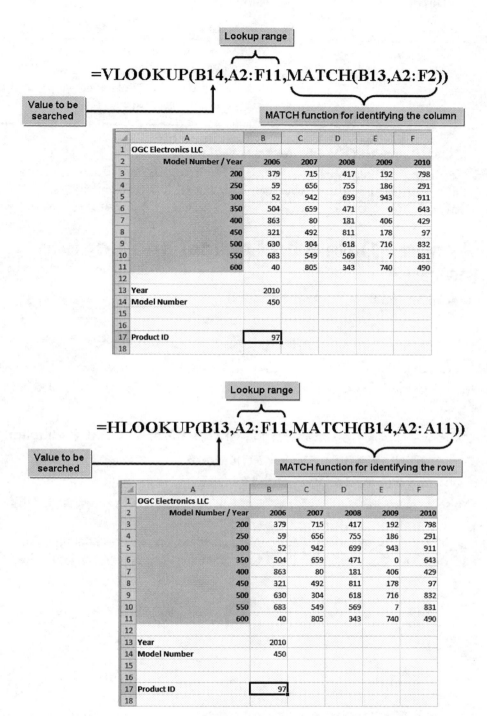

Figure 1-5: *Searching for values using the VLOOKUP and HLOOKUP functions.*

The VLOOKUP and HLOOKUP functions consist of the following arguments.

Argument	Purpose
Lookup_value	A number or text value that the function will use to look for along the top row of the table array.
Table_array	The block of information the function will search.

Argument	Purpose
Row_index_num or Col_index_num	The row or column number indicating where the function will go to return the data.
Range_lookup	A value that specifies whether you want to find an exact or approximate match.

Syntax for VLOOKUP and HLOOKUP Functions

The syntax for the VLOOKUP function is: VLOOKUP(lookup_value, table_array, col_index_num, range_lookup). The syntax for the HLOOKUP function is: HLOOKUP(lookup_value, table_array, row_index_num, range_lookup).

How to Analyze Data with Logical and Lookup Functions

Procedure Reference: Insert a Logical Function

To insert a logical function in a worksheet:

1. Select the cell into which the function will be placed.

2. Enter the logical function.

3. If necessary, in the **Function Arguments** dialog box, enter the arguments required and then click **OK.**

Procedure Reference: Look Up Data with the HLOOKUP or VLOOKUP Function

To look up data with the HLOOKUP or VLOOKUP function:

1. Select the cell into which the HLOOKUP or VLOOKUP function will be placed.

2. Using the formula entry method of your choice, enter the HLOOKUP or VLOOKUP function name.

3. Using the argument entry method of your choice, enter the arguments: Lookup value; Table Array; Row index number or Column Index Number; and Range Lookup value (optional).

4. If necessary, press Enter to complete the entry of the function.

ACTIVITY 1-4
Entering Functions that Apply Logical Analysis

Data Files:

Employee Bonus.xlsx

Scenario:

Heading the sales team at OGC Bookstores, you have recommended a compensation structure such that a 1% bonus will be given to all salespersons who meet their targets. Additionally, a bonus of 1% will be given for each business with sales greater than $115,000. If employees exceed their set targets and get a bonus in two or more business categories, they will be rewarded with a President's Club vacation. You want to create an Excel sheet for processing this data and want to demonstrate it to the human resources manager.

---

1. Enter a function to calculate the goal bonus for all employees.

   a. From the C:\084577Data\Calculating Data with Advanced Formulas folder, open the Employee Bonus.xlsx file.

   b. Select cell **I7,** type *=IF()* and on the **Formulas** tab, in the **Function Library** group, click **Insert Function.**

   c. In the **Function Arguments** dialog box, in the **Logical_test** text box, type *F7>=G7*

   d. In the **Value_if_true** text box, type *F7*$H$4*

   e. In the **Value_if_false** text box, type *0* and click **OK.**

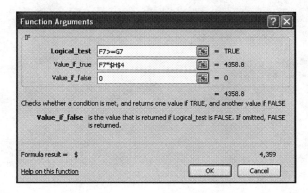

   f. Fill in the formula for the range **I8:I12** to calculate the goal bonus for all other employees.

g. Observe that goal bonuses have been given to three employees.

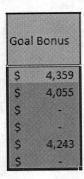

Goal Bonus
$ 4,359
$ 4,055
$ -
$ -
$ 4,243
$ -

2. Enter a formula to calculate the Category Bonus for the employees.

a. Select cell **J7** and type **=$H$4*SUMIF(**

b. Click **Insert Function.**

c. In the **Function Arguments** dialog box, in the **Range** text box, type **B7:E7**

d. In the **Criteria** text box, type **>115000** and click **OK.**

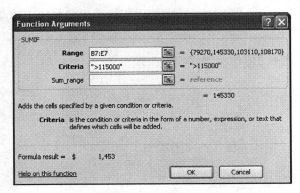

e. Fill in the formula for all the other employees.

f. Notice that all employees except Jamie received a category bonus.

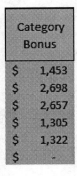

Category Bonus
$ 1,453
$ 2,698
$ 2,657
$ 1,305
$ 1,322
$ -

3. Enter a function to calculate the number of times each employee received a bonus for a category.

a. Select cell **K7** and enter **=COUNTIF(B7:E7,">115000")**

b.   Fill in the formula for all the other employees.

4.   Enter a function to display information on whether or not an employee is invited to the President's Club.

a.   Scroll to the right, in cell **M7**, enter *=IF(AND(I7>0,K7>1),"President's Club", "")*

b.   Fill in the formula for all the other employees.

c.   Observe that the formula displays only one of the employees being invited to the President's Club.

Number of Category Bonus Hits	Total Compensation	Honor
1	$ 23,247	
2	$ 22,973	President's Club
2	$ 18,577	
1	$ 15,588	
1	$ 22,537	
0	$ 7,546	

d.   Save the file as **My Employee Bonus** and then close it.

ACTIVITY 1-5
Locating Part Numbers with the HLOOKUP and VLOOKUP Functions

Data Files:

Product IDs.xlsx

Scenario:

You are responsible for managing the customer service department of OGC Electronics LLC, a company selling electronic equipment. When a customer calls in, the customer service employee needs to quickly have the product ID available in order to help the customer. You identified the need of creating a file for your department that would enable them to quickly have the IDs available for all products. The customer will provide the year and model number, and your worksheet should determine the correct product ID.

1. Enter the formula to search the product ID using VLOOKUP function.

    a. From C:\084577Data\Calculating Data with Advanced Formulas folder, open the Product IDs.xlsx file.

    b. Observe the value in cell **M14**.

    c. Scroll to the left and then scroll down and in cell **B77**, enter **2010**

    d. In cell **B78**, type **750**

    e. Click cell **B80** and enter **=VLOOKUP(B78,A2:M75,MATCH(B77,A2:M2))** to search the product ID based on model number.

    f. Observe that the correct product ID **974** is displayed in the cell **B80**.

    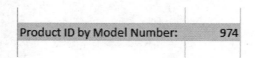

     The product ID can also be searched by using the HLOOKUP formula. HLOOKUP will search the table by the Year name. The formula in this case would be **=HLOOKUP(B77,A2:M75,MATCH(B78,A2:A75))**

    g. Save the file as **My Product IDs** and close it

2. **True or False? The VLOOKUP function retrieves information from the columns that contain the value being searched.**

    __ True

    __ False

Lesson 1 Follow-up

In this lesson, you solved mathematical problems by calculating with advanced formulas. There are occasions when you may require a large number of formulas to be used. In such situations, using advanced functions will help you find the correct solution quickly.

1. **What types of advanced calculations have you encountered either on the job or personally?**

2. **What factors will influence the choice of a range name?**

2 | Organizing Worksheet and Table Data

Lesson Time: 1 hour(s), 30 minutes

Lesson Objectives:

In this lesson, you will organize worksheet and table data using various techniques.

You will:

- Create and modify tables.
- Format tables.
- Sort or filter worksheet or table data.
- Use functions to calculate data.

Introduction

In the previous lesson, you performed advanced calculations on data in worksheets. These calculations and other data-management functions become even easier when you use the data organization tools that Microsoft® Office Excel® provides. In this lesson, you will organize worksheet and table data.

For information to be clearly understood, you must present it in a logical and coherent structure. Unless data is presented in a logical manner, it loses its value, rendering the information useless. On the other hand, if you organize your worksheet and table data clearly, you can help make the data come to life for you and for others who use the information.

TOPIC A

Create and Modify Tables

In this lesson, you will organize worksheet and table data. Creating a table is one of the best ways of organizing data. In this topic, you will create tables for a set of data.

While Excel data is organized into rows and columns, the data specific to your needs will not be treated as a unique data set on the worksheet unless you represent it using tables. Organizing data into tables would allow you to apply unique formatting options, thereby making the data distinct from the rest of the worksheet and improving its clarity.

Tables

Definition:

A *table* is a collection of contiguous rows and columns within a worksheet that Excel treats as an independent data set as compared to the rest of worksheet. A table within an Excel worksheet can be formatted, managed, and analyzed as a discrete object. Using a table instead of an ordinary range to hold worksheet data makes some worksheet operations easier, and also provides some table-specific functions and formatting options. Tables can have headers for rows and columns that help users to identify the information displayed in them. Tables can contain any number of rows and columns depending on the available data, though cells within a table can also be left blank.

Example:

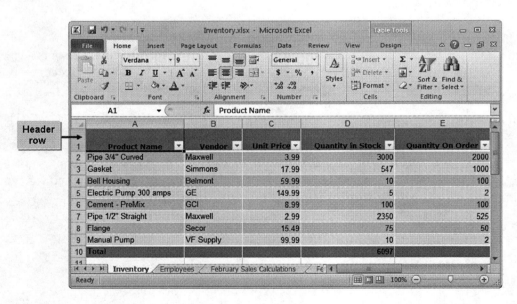

Figure 2-1: *Presenting data in the tabular format makes it easier to understand.*

Table Components

A table contains different components that can be used to enhance a presentation.

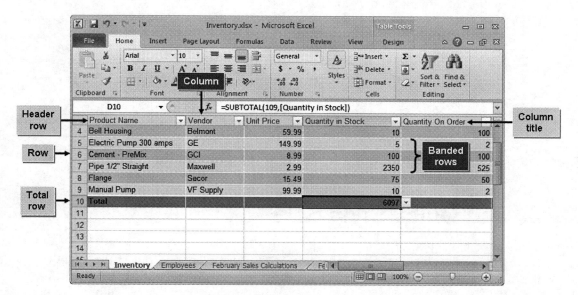

Figure 2-2: *The various components of a table.*

Component	Description
Table title	The name of the table. The table name can be edited so that you can refer to it while using formulas.
Row	A horizontal array of cells within the table holding data.
Column	A vertical array of cells within the table holding data.
Header row	The first row in a table that contains labels. Column header cells have filter drop-down arrows by which data can be filtered and sorted.
Total row	The last row in a table that displays the total or other summary data for each column. Cells in the total row have drop-down lists that you can use to select common table formulas. The default formula is to subtotal the column.
Banded row	The formatting of rows differentiating even numbered rows from odd numbered rows.
Banded column	The formatting of columns differentiating even numbered columns from odd numbered columns.

The Create Table Dialog Box

The **Create Table** dialog box enables you to select a range of data to create a table. It also gives you the option of adding headers to tables.

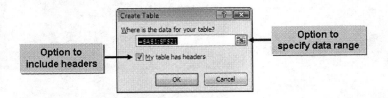

Figure 2-3: *The Create Table dialog box is used to create a new table.*

Styles and Quick Style Sets

A *style* is a named collection of formatting options that you can apply as a group. A *Quick Style set* is a group of styles selected to coordinate with each other and reflect the overall theme of a worksheet. There are different Quick Style sets for different object types, such as tables and cells. The Quick Styles for each object appear in a gallery on the Ribbon. By placing the mouse pointer over a thumbnail in the Quick Style gallery, you can see a live preview of how the selected object would look if the Quick Style is applied.

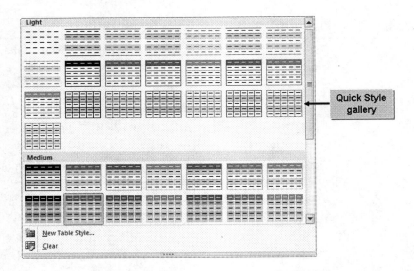

Figure 2-4: *The various Quick Styles available in Excel.*

The Table Tools Design Contextual Tab

The **Table Tools Design** contextual tab is displayed when a table is selected. It contains tools to design tables in a worksheet.

Group	Description
Properties	Enables you to resize the table and edit the table name.
Tools	Provides you with options to create PivotTables, convert a table into a range of cells, and check for duplicate data.
External Table Data	Enables you to share data with external programs as well as automatically update the workbook with external data. Further, you can also unlink the external source from your table.
Table Style Options	Enables you to format and modify your table by adding or removing the header or total row, banding rows or columns, and formatting the first or last column separately.
Table Styles	Enables you to apply predefined table styles to your document.

Table Modification Options

After you create a table in a worksheet, you can use various methods to modify the structure of the table without affecting the surrounding worksheet data. You can easily insert or delete individual rows or columns within the table boundaries without affecting data across the entire worksheet. You can change the overall size of the table to automatically add or remove rows and columns and apply the table formatting to the new table range as needed. If you have duplicate data in any of the table columns, you can remove those rows, leaving only unique values in any given column. You can also convert a table to a normal data range if you want to remove the table functionality while preserving the worksheet data and the applied table formatting.

How to Create and Modify Tables

Procedure Reference: Create a Table with the Default Table Style

To create a table with the default table style:

1. On the **Ribbon**, select the **Insert** tab.
2. In the **Tables** group, click **Table** to display the **Create Table** dialog box.
3. Specify the data range for the table.
   - In the **Where Is The Data For Your Table** text box, type the data range.
   - Or, in the worksheet, select the data range.
4. If necessary, in the **Create Table** dialog box, check the **My Table Has Headers** check box to use the first row of data in the table range as the column headers. If you uncheck this box, Excel will use default column header names such as Column1 and Column2.
5. In the **Create Table** dialog box, click **OK.**

Procedure Reference: Create a Table with a Selected Table Style

To create a table with a selected table style:

1. If you have a range of data you want to create as a table, select the range.

2. On the **Home** tab, in the **Styles** group, click **Format As Table.**

3. In the gallery, select a table style.

4. In the **Format As Table** dialog box, enter or verify the data range in the **Where Is The Data For Your Table** text box.

5. If necessary, check the **My Table Has Headers** check box, and then click **OK.**

Procedure Reference: Convert a Table to a Worksheet Data Range

To convert a table to a worksheet data range:

1. Select a cell in the table to display the **Table Tools Design** contextual tab on the **Ribbon.** (If necessary, on the **Ribbon**, select the **Table Tools Design** contextual tab.)

2. In the **Tools** group, click **Convert To Range.**

3. In the message box, click **Yes** to convert the table to a normal range.

 To delete table contents and remove the table at the same time, select the table and press **Delete**, or click **Delete** in the **Cells** group on the **Home** tab.

Procedure Reference: Add or Delete Table Rows and Columns

To add or delete table rows and columns:

1. Select a cell or cells in the table.

2. Add or delete table rows or columns.

- To add rows or columns, on the **Home** tab, in the **Cells** group, click the **Insert** drop-down arrow, or right-click the selection and choose **Insert** to add rows or columns.

- The insert options that appear will depend on the position and size of the range you selected within the table. Choose the appropriate option to insert rows above or below the selection, or columns to the left or right of the selection.

- To delete rows or columns, on the **Home** tab, in the **Cells** group, click the **Delete** drop-down arrow and select **Delete Table Rows** or **Delete Table Columns**, or right-click the selection and choose **Delete→Delete Table Rows** or **Delete→Delete Table Columns.**

Procedure Reference: Resize a Table

To resize a table by specifying a different range:

1. Select a cell in the table.

2. If necessary, on the **Ribbon**, select the **Table Tools Design** contextual tab.

3. In the **Properties** group, click **Resize Table.**

4. Specify the new table range.

- In the worksheet, click and drag to specify the range of the table.

- Or, in the **Resize Table** dialog box, type the new range.

5. In the **Resize Table** dialog box, click **OK** to modify the table.

Procedure Reference: Remove Duplicate Rows in a Table

To remove table rows that contain duplicate data:

1. Select a cell in the table.

2. If necessary, on the **Ribbon**, select the **Table Tools Design** contextual tab.

3. In the **Tools** group, click **Remove Duplicates.**

4. In the **Remove Duplicates** dialog box, specify the desired settings.

   - Check the **My Data Has Headers** check box to treat the user-defined names as headers.

   - Click **Select All** to include all the fields in the table for locating duplicate values.

   - Click **Unselect All** to deselect all the selected fields, and then in the **Columns** list box, check only the desired fields for locating duplicate values.

5. Click **OK.**

6. In the message box, click **OK** to remove duplicate rows, or to close the message box if there are no duplicates.

ACTIVITY 2-1
Creating and Manipulating Tables

Data Files:

Inventory.xlsx

Scenario:

You are responsible for the management of inventory for OGC Constructions. You need to present the data related to existing inventory to the board members for accounting purpose. You want to draw attention to certain portions of the data and have decided to convert the data into a table to take advantage of the flexibility of formatting in tables.

1. Convert the data on the Inventory sheet into a table.

   a. From the C:\084577Data\Organizing Worksheet and Table Data folder, open the Inventory.xlsx file.

   b. On the **Inventory** sheet, verify that there are no blank columns between column **A** and **F**. Scroll to the right.

   c. Verify that there are no blank columns between columns **J** and **L**.

   d. Scroll to the left and select any cell within the first set of data to be tabled.

   e. On the **Insert** tab, in the **Tables** group, click **Table**.

   f. In the **Create Table** dialog box, verify that the table range is listed as **=$A$1:$F$18**, and the **My table has headers** option is checked. Click **OK**.

   g. Observe that the selected range of cells is displayed as a table with column headers, filter drop-down arrows, and banded rows for easy readability.

h.   On the **Table Tools Design** contextual tab, in the **Table Style Options** group, verify that the **Header row** and **Banded Rows** check boxes are checked.

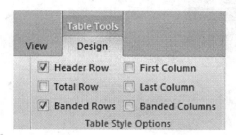

i.   On the **Table Tools Design** contextual tab, in the **Table Styles** group, verify that the fourth style from left is applied to the table by default.

j.   Similarly insert a table for the data in the range **J1:L22** of the same worksheet.

2.   Delete a product from the **Inventory** table and insert a new row for the item "grout".

a.   Scroll to the left and in the first table, select cell **A12.**

b.   Scroll to the right.

c.   Observe the data in row **12** of the second table is related to the product named "Pipe 3/4″ Curved."

d.   On the **Home** tab, in the **Cells** group, click the **Delete** drop-down and select **Delete Table Rows.**

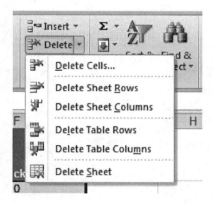

e.   Verify that the data related to "Pipe 3/4″ Curved" in row **12** of the second table remains unchanged even though row **12** is deleted in table 1.

f.   With cell **A12** selected, in the **Cells** group, click the **Insert** drop-down and select **Insert Table Rows Above.**

g.   Enter the following new product information in row 12.
   ● A12: Grout
   ● B12: 3M
   ● C12: 2.49
   ● D12: 250
   ● E12: 75

- F12: 0

Caulk - White	3M	6.99
Grout	3M	2.49
Tiles - quarter-cut	Tile Place	4.99
Tiles - third-cut	Tile Place	8.99

---

3. Insert an Order Date column in the table.

    a. Select cell **F3.**

    b. In the **Cells** group, click the **Insert** drop-down and choose **Insert Table Columns to the Left.**

    c. Observe that the **Microsoft Excel** message box is displayed, advising you against the addition of columns in the table as that would disrupt the data in the second table due to the shifting of cells. Click **OK.**

    d. Create a new worksheet, remove the second table from the **Inventory** sheet and place it on the new worksheet. Rename the new worksheet as *Product ID*

    e. In the **Inventory** sheet, select cell **F3**, in the **Cells** group, click the **Insert** drop-down and select **Insert Table Columns to the Left.**

    f. Select cell **F1** and enter *Order Date*

    g. Navigate to the C:\084577Data\Organizing Worksheet and Table Data folder and copy the data from the Dates.txt file and paste it in the **Order Date** column.

Order Date
4/7/2010
4/14/2010
4/15/2010
4/13/2010
5/3/2010
5/4/2010
5/5/2010
5/6/2010
5/7/2010
5/17/2010
5/18/2010
5/19/2010
5/20/2010
5/26/2010
5/27/2010
4/7/2010
5/29/2010

    h. Close the Dates.txt file.

---

4. Remove duplicate rows from the table.

    a. Observe that rows **2** and **17** in the Inventory table have duplicate data. Select cell **F2** and then select the **Table Tools Design** contextual tab.

b.   In the **Tools** group, click **Remove Duplicates.**

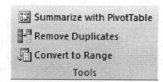

c.   In the **Remove Duplicates** dialog box, verify that the **My data has headers** check box and all the columns are checked, and click **OK.**

d.   In the **Microsoft Excel** message box, click **OK** to remove the duplicate values.

e.   Observe that the second instance of the duplicate data has been removed from the table.

f.   Save the file as *My Inventory*

TOPIC B

Format Tables

In the previous topic, you created and modified tables. Once you have established the structure of your table, you can apply table-specific formatting options and customize the table format. In this topic, you will format tables.

A table that uses the default format might not be visually appealing to you, and the information might not be clearly identifiable. Customizing the formatting enables you to present data effectively and draw the reader's eye to the important information in the table. The table formatting tools in Excel enable you to customize the format of an individual table, as well as save your custom table formats so that you can apply them to all tables in your worksheet.

How to Format Tables

Procedure Reference: Format a Table

To format a table:

1. In the worksheet, select any part of the table.
2. If necessary, on the **Ribbon**, select the **Table Tools Design** contextual tab.
3. To apply a table style, select the desired table style from the **Table Styles** group.
4. To modify the applied style, in the **Table Styles Options** group, check or uncheck the desired check boxes. Both the table appearance and the preview of the applied style in the **Quick Styles** gallery will change to match the options you select.
5. If necessary, to remove a table style, in the **Table Styles** group, click the **More** button and select **Clear.**
6. To format individual cells or portions of the table, use the cell formatting options on the **Home** tab.

Procedure Reference: Create a Custom Table Style

To create a custom table style:

1. Select any part of the table.
2. Display the **New Table Quick Style** dialog box.
   - On the **Table Tools Design** contextual tab, in the **Table Styles** group, click the **More** button and select **New Table Style.**
   - Or, on the **Home** tab, in the **Styles** group, click **Format As Table** and select **New Table Style.**
3. In the **New Table Quick Style** dialog box, in the **Name** text box, type a name for the custom table style.
4. Format the desired table element.
   a. In the **Table Element** list box, select a table element and click **Format.**
   b. In the **Format Cells** dialog box, select the desired tab to select the font, border, and fill for the custom table style.
   c. If necessary, on the desired tab, click **Clear** to remove the selected formatting.
   d. Click **OK.**
5. If necessary, repeat step 4 to format other table elements.

6. If necessary, in the **New Table Quick Styles** dialog box, click **Clear** to remove the formatting for the selected table element.

7. If necessary, from the **Stripe Size** drop-down list, select the desired stripe size.

8. If desired, check the **Set As Default Table Quick Style For This Document** check box to make the custom table style the default table style.

9. Click **OK** to create the custom table style.

Procedure Reference: Delete a Custom Table Style

To delete a custom table style:

1. Open the worksheet with the custom table style, and select any part of the table.

2. Display the **Table Styles** gallery.

   - On the **Table Tools Design** contextual tab, in the **Table Styles** group, click **More.**

   - On the **Home** tab, in the **Styles** group, click **Format As Table.**

3. In the **Custom** section, right-click the custom table style to be removed and choose **Delete.**

4. Click **OK** in the message box to confirm the deletion of the custom style.

Using Custom Styles in Other Workbooks

By default, a custom style is saved in the workbook in which it is created, and is not available in other workbooks. To use a custom table style in another workbook, copy a table that has the custom style applied into another workbook, and save the target workbook.

ACTIVITY 2-2
Formatting a Table

Data Files:

New Employees List.xlsx

Scenario:

Your company has assigned employee IDs and extensions to new employees who have completed their training. The employees' office locations have also been finalized. You decide to put the data in an Excel table, which will be forwarded to all the employees concerned. To ensure a better visual appeal, you have decided to format the table.

1. Change the font size, text alignment, and border color of the table.

   a. From the C:\084577Data\Organizing Worksheet and Table Data folder, open the New Employees List.xlsx file.

   b. Select the range **A1:F1** to select the header row of the table.

   c. On the **Home** tab, in the **Font** group, from the **Font Size** drop-down, select **12**, and in the **Alignment** group, click **Center**.

   d. Select the entire table. In the **Font** group, click the **Bottom Border** drop-down, and select **More Borders.**

   e. In the **Format Cells** dialog box, in the **Line** section, from the **Color** drop-down list, under the **Theme Colors** section, select **Blue, Accent 1**, the fifth color from the left on the first row.

   f. In the **Presets** section, click **Outline** and **Inside**, and click **OK.**

   g. Click outside the table to view the borders.

2. Apply a different color style to the table.

   a. Click inside the table to display the **Table Tools Design** contextual tab.

   b. In the **Table Styles** group, click the **More** button, and in the **Medium** section, select **Table Style Medium 2**, the second option in the first row.

   c. Save the file as *My New Employees List*

ACTIVITY 2-3
Creating a Custom Table Style

Setup:

My New Employees List is open.

Scenario:

After formatting the New Employees List table, you feel that you could have enhanced the worksheet further. You create a new custom style that specifies the desired color for the header and the body of the table. Also, you format the pre-existing font and border colors of the table to suit the new custom style.

1. Display the **New Table Quick Style** dialog box.

    a. On the **Table Tools Design** contextual tab, in the **Table Styles** group, click the **More** button to display the Table Styles gallery.

    b. Select **New Table Style.**

2. Select the formatting options for the table elements.

    a. In the **New Table Quick Style** dialog box, in the **Name** text box, type *My Table Style*

    b. In the **Table Element** list box, select **Header Row** and click **Format.**

    c. On the **Font** tab, from the **Font style** list box, select **Bold.**

    d. In the **Format Cells** dialog box, on the **Fill** tab, in the **Background Color** section, from the fifth row, select the third color from the right and click **OK.**

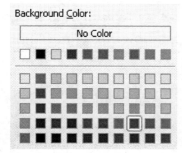

    e. In the **Table Element** list box, select **First Row Stripe** and click **Format.**

f. In the **Format Cells** dialog box, on the **Fill** tab, in the **Background Color** section, in the third row, select the third color from the right and click **OK.**

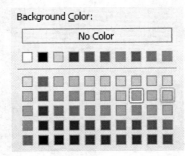

g. In the **Table Element** list box, select **Second Row Stripe** and click **Format.**

h. In the **Format Cells** dialog box, on the **Fill** tab, in the **Background Color** section, in the second row, select the third color from the right and click **OK.**

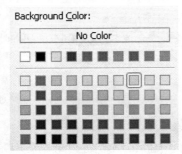

i. In the **New Table Quick Style** dialog box, click **OK** to save the new style.

3. Apply the newly created custom table style to the table.

a. On the **Table Tools Design** contextual tab, in the **Table Styles** group, click the **More** button.

b. In the **Table Styles** gallery, under **Custom**, select **My Table Style** to apply the custom table style to the table.

4. Format the font and border colors to match the custom table style.

a. Select the cell range **A1:F1.**

b. On the **Home** tab, in the **Font** group, from the **Font Color** drop-down, in the **Theme Colors** section, in the first row, select **White, Background 1,** the first color in the first row.

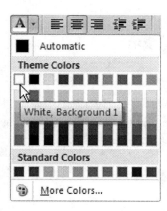

c. Click outside the table to view the font color in the header row.

d. Select the entire table.

e. In the **Font** group, from the **More Borders** drop-down, choose **More Borders.**

f. In the **Format Cells** dialog box, in the **Line** section, from the **Color** drop-down list, in the **Theme Colors** section, in the fifth row, select the third color from the right.

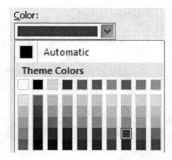

g. In the **Presets** section, click **Outline** and **Inside** and click **OK.**

h. Click outside the table to view the borders.

i. Save the file and close it.

TOPIC C
Sort or Filter Data

In the previous topics, you created and modified tables. Once you have created a table, it is easy to manipulate table data by sorting or filtering it. With a few more steps, you can sort or filter worksheet data ranges as well. In this topic, you will sort or filter worksheet or table data.

After you enter data in your worksheet, you may want to view the data in a different way. When you sort data, you can create different views of the same data without altering its original format. Filtering the data will help you to eliminate unnecessary data from appearing on your worksheet.

Sorting

Definition:

A *sort* is a method of viewing data arranged in a specific order. Data can be sorted in either *ascending order* or *descending order* based on the type of information it contains: numeric or alphabetic. Data can be sorted on a single criterion or multiple criteria. You can sort data within tables or within ordinary worksheet data ranges.

Example: Single Level Sort: Ascending Order

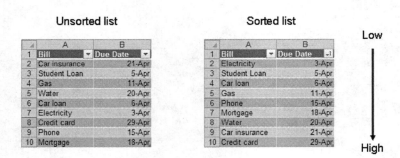

Figure 2-5: A single level sort applies the same sorting criteria to all rows and columns.

Example: Multiple Level Sort: Ascending and Descending Orders

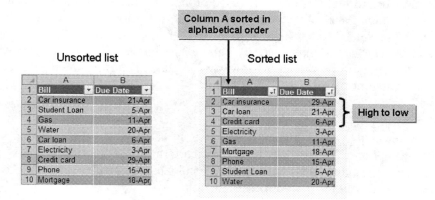

Multiple level sort

Figure 2-6: A multiple level sort allows different rows or columns to be sorted according to different criteria.

Filters

Definition:

A *filter* is a method of viewing only the data that meets a criterion. Data can be filtered on a single criterion or multiple criteria using numeric and alphabetic information. When data does not meet the filter criteria, the entire row is hidden. A filter can rearrange data in the current table or worksheet range, or copy information to another location. You can restore the filtered data to its original format by removing the filter.

Example:

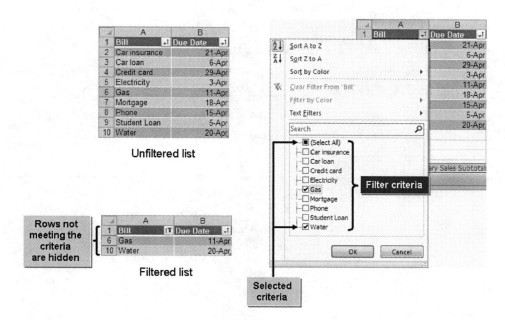

Figure 2-7: Filters allow users to view only the required data.

AutoFilter

One of the most useful features in Excel is AutoFilter, a drop-down located at the bottom-right corner of each column label in the header row. AutoFilter allows you to filter the displayed data according to a set criterion, such as in increasing or decreasing order or displaying only those rows that meet the specified criteria. This feature can be activated or removed by using the **Filter** button in the **Sort & Filter** group on the **Data** tab. You can specify the filtering criteria using the **Custom AutoFilter** dialog box.

Search Filter

The Search Filter helps you to efficiently find data in large worksheets by using instant search in your filtering options. Even as you type a search term in the **Search** text box, all relevant items are instantly displayed and the displayed results can be further filtered. The Search Filter is available in the AutoFilter drop-down of the column.

The Advanced Filter Dialog Box

The **Advanced Filter** dialog box is an extension to the filtering capabilities of Excel and allows users to apply complex filtering criteria to tables. You can use it to eliminate duplicate values from getting displayed within the specified range. You can also use it to copy the filtering criteria to multiple ranges within the same worksheet or to other worksheets.

Filter Operators

You can use any of the several filter operators to fine-tune a data filter.

Filter Operator	Used To
"=text"	Find the exact text specified within the quotation marks.
?	Replace any single character in the same position as the question mark.
*	Replace multiple characters in the same position as the asterisk.
=	Find values equal to the filter criterion.
<	Find values less than the filter criterion.
>	Find values greater than the filter criterion.
=<	Find values equal to or less than the filter criterion.
=>	Find values equal to or greater than the filter criterion.
<>	Find values not equal to the filter criterion.

How to Sort or Filter Worksheet or Table Data

Procedure Reference: Sort Data in Worksheet Ranges

To sort data in worksheet ranges:

1. Select any cell in the worksheet range.

2. To perform a quick sort on the selected column, on the **Data** tab, in the **Sort & Filter** group, click the appropriate ascending or descending sort button.

   The screentip description of the buttons will change depending on the data in the selected column.

3. To create custom sort criteria, on the **Data** tab, in the **Sort & Filter** group, click **Sort.**

4. In the **Sort** dialog box, from the **Sort By** drop-down list, select the column you want to sort by.

5. If necessary, from the **Sort On** drop-down list, select the item you want to sort on.
   - **Values**
   - **Cell Color**
   - **Font Color**
   - **Cell Icon**

6. If necessary, from the **Order** drop-down list, select the ordering you desire.

7. If desired, click **Add Level** to add another sort level for a multiple-level sort.

8. If necessary, from the **Then By** drop-down list, select the column you want to sort by.

9. If necessary, select the items you want to sort on and select the ordering you desire.

10. Click **OK.**

Procedure Reference: Sort Data in a Table

To sort data in a table:

1. Click the drop-down arrow in the column heading that you want to sort by.

2. Select the sort option based on the data in the column. For numeric columns, you can sort from highest to lowest or vice-versa. For text columns, you can sort from A to Z or from Z to A. For date columns, you can sort from oldest to newest or vice-versa.

3. To create custom sort criteria, click **Sort By Color→Custom Sort** to open the **Sort** dialog box.

4. In the **Sort** dialog box, choose the column to be sorted, the value to be used for sorting, and the order of sort and then click **OK.**

Procedure Reference: Filter Data in a Table or Worksheet Range

To filter data in a table or a worksheet range:

1. If the data is in a worksheet range, select any cell in the range and, on the **Data** tab, in the **Sort & Filter** group, click **Filter** to activate the filter drop-down lists.

2. On the column you want to use as a filter criterion, click the **Filter** drop-down list button.

3. Check or uncheck check boxes to select filter criteria based on the data in the column and click **OK.**

4. To set advanced filter criteria, open the **Filter** drop-down list, select **Text Filters** or **Number Filters** and then choose the desired filter criterion. Configure the filter in the **Custom AutoFilter** dialog box and click **OK.**

5. To remove the filter, click the **Filter** drop-down list and select **Clear Filter From "[column name]"**.

Procedure Reference: Using the Advanced Filter Dialog Box

To use the **Advanced Filter** dialog box to set additional filter criteria:

1. Select a cell in the table.

2. On the **Data** tab, in the **Sort & Filter** group, click **Advanced.**

3. In the **Advanced Filter** dialog box, in the **List range** text box, enter the list range of your choice.

4. In the **Criteria range** text box, enter the range for which you want to apply the filtering criteria.

5. If necessary, check the **Unique record only** check box to retain only unique values in the specified list range.

6. If necessary, select **Copy to another location** to activate the **Copy to** text, and in the text box, enter the range to which the criteria must be copied.

7. Click **OK.**

ACTIVITY 2-4
Sorting and Filtering Tables

Before You Begin:

My Inventory.xlsx is open.

Scenario:

You have to submit an inventory report to the accounts manager for auditing. You have already created the report, but the manager wants the report to be sorted based on the quantity in stock for each product in descending order. The manager also wants a report on the products that were purchased before May. You decide to sort the data in the existing report and apply filters to display the products that were purchased before May.

1. Sort the table data in the decreasing order of the Quantity in Stock.

   a. Select cell **D1,** and on the **Data** tab, in the **Sort & Filter** group, click **Sort.**

   b. In the **Sort** dialog box, from the **Sort by** drop-down list, select **Quantity in Stock.**

   c. From the **Order** drop down list, select **Largest to Smallest** and click **OK.**

2. Apply filters to display the products that were purchased before May.

   a. Observe that the table rows are rearranged in the decreasing order of quantity in stock. Click the drop-down arrow in cell **F1** and choose **Date Filters→Before.**

   b. In the **Custom AutoFilter** dialog box, in the drop-down list adjacent to the **is before** drop-down list, choose **5/3/2010** and click **OK.**

   c. Observe that the report displays only those products that were purchased before May.

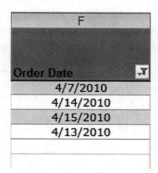

   d. Click the **Filter** button for **Order Date.**

   e. Select **Clear Filter From "Order Date"** to display all the rows.

   f. Save the file as *My Sorted Inventory* and close it.

TOPIC D
Use Functions to Calculate Data

In the previous topic, you sorted and filtered data in worksheets and tables. Instead of just rearranging the worksheet or table data, you might want to perform calculations on it. In this topic, you will perform calculations on tables and worksheet data ranges.

When you use a formula to perform a calculation in a worksheet, you have to choose the data you want included in the calculation. This can take some time if there is a large amount of data. Database functions and other types of summary functions, on the other hand, can find the data you are looking for and perform the calculation all in one step.

Summary Functions in Tables

If your table has a totals row, you can use the drop-down list for each total cell to insert summary results for that column of the table. The drop-down list displays common summary operations such as Sum or Average; no matter which function you select, Excel places the SUBTOTAL function in the totals cell. The first argument of the SUBTOTAL function is a reference number that indicates which specific summary function Excel will calculate for that cell; for example, the reference number 101 produces an average. The other arguments in the SUBTOTAL function give the data ranges for the calculation.

 For a complete list of the function number code references for the SUBTOTAL function, see the Excel Help system.

Database Functions

Definition:

A *database function* is a function that performs a calculation only on data that meets certain criteria. Each database function starts with the letter D. A database function has three arguments: the database, the field, and the criteria. The *database* is a worksheet data range or a table. The *field* is the column within the database that you want to perform calculations on. The *criteria* is a range of cells in the worksheet that contains column names and data that specify the information you want to locate within the database. The criteria range must contain at least two cells, one with a field name and one with data, but you can use multiple columns and rows within the criteria range to create complex database queries.

Example:

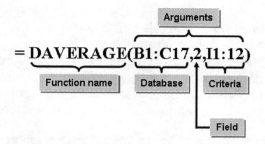

Figure 2-8: A database function has three arguments.

AND and OR Conditions

Definition:

AND conditions and *OR conditions* are methods for including multiple criteria in a criteria range to control its restrictiveness. In an AND condition, the criteria is displayed in multiple columns on the same row in the criteria range. The results of the query must meet the first criterion in the row, *and* the second criterion, and so forth. In an OR condition, the criteria is displayed in multiple rows in the criteria range. The results of the query can meet the criteria on the first row, *or* the criteria on the second row, and so forth. You can combine AND and OR conditions in a criteria range.

Example:

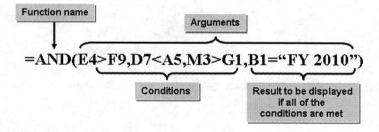

Figure 2-9: A function containing the AND condition.

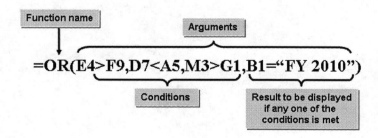

Figure 2-10: A function containing the OR condition.

Subtotals

Definition:

A *subtotal* is an operation performed on a subset of data in a sorted worksheet data range. The sorted data creates a separate group at each change in the sort field. The subtotal can be created using several functions such as SUM, AVERAGE, and COUNT, though the default subtotal function is SUM. A worksheet can have as many subtotals as required, and each subtotal is inserted in the worksheet on a separate line below the group that is being subtotaled. The subtotals are then added to create a grand total at the end of the data list.

 You cannot subtotal tables. If you need to subtotal table data, you will need to convert the table to a data range.

Example:

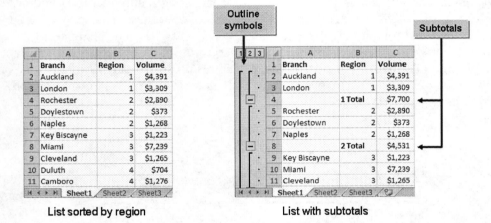

List sorted by region   List with subtotals

Figure 2-11: *Subtotal allows you to split the total amount into smaller parts.*

How to Use Functions to Calculate Data

Procedure Reference: Change the Summary Function of the Total Row in a Table

To change the summary function of any cell of the total row in a table:

1. Select the cell in the Total row of the desired column.

2. Click the drop-down arrow in that cell and choose the desired summary function from the list.

Procedure Reference: Insert the DSUM, DCOUNT, or DAVERAGE Database Function

To insert the DSUM, DCOUNT, or DAVERAGE database function:

1. Select the cell into which you want to place the function.

2. Use the method you prefer to insert the function and open the **Function Arguments** dialog box.

3. In the **Function Arguments** dialog box, in the **Database** argument field, select the range or specify the table that contains all the data you want the function to process. Be sure to include the column headings in the range if any are present.

4. In the **Field** argument field, enter the column number or column header name of the column you want to calculate.

5. In the **Criteria** argument field, enter the range where you plan to enter criteria information and click **OK**.

 A best practice for creating the criteria range is to copy the column headings for the main data table and paste them to another location of the spreadsheet where there is enough room to add the criteria variables in the row under the pasted headings.

6. Enter the criteria in the criteria range cells to see the results of the function.

Overlaying Criteria Ranges

You can overlay criteria ranges on the same cells for multiple database functions such as DAVERAGE, DCOUNT, and DSUM.

Procedure Reference: Insert Subtotals in a Data Range

To insert subtotals in a data range:

1. If the data is in a table, convert the table to a range.

   a. Select any cell in the table.

   b. On the **Table Tools Design** contextual tab, in the **Tools** group, click **Convert To Range.**

   c. In the message box, click **Yes** to convert the table to a named range.

2. Select any cell in the data range in which you want to insert subtotals.

3. On the **Data** tab, in the **Outline** group, click **Subtotal.**

4. If necessary, in the **Subtotal** dialog box, from the **At Each Change In** drop-down list, select the column heading containing the sorted information whose duplicates will be grouped into subtotals.

5. If necessary, from the **Use Function** drop-down list, select the function to use in the subtotal.

6. If necessary, in the **Add Subtotal To** list box, verify that the check boxes next to the column headings you want to be subtotaled are checked, and, if necessary, check or uncheck them.

7. If necessary, include or remove the additional settings depending on the output results you desire.

   - **Replace Current Subtotals**
   - **Page Break Between Groups**
   - **Summary Below Data**

8. Click **OK.**

ACTIVITY 2-5
Applying Calculations to a Table or Worksheet

Data Files:

Quarter 1 Sales.xlsx

Scenario:

As the regional sales manager for OGC Bookstores (North American region), you are required to provide estimations based on the sales of the past three months to the sales manager. The sales manager also wants to know the total sales and average sales for each month of the quarter. He has specifically asked for a list of days when total sales were less than $1000 in all the regions. Later, he requests a list of days when any one on the regions had sales totaling less than $500.

1. Calculate the total and average sales for a month.

    a. From the C:\084577Data\Organizing Worksheet and Table Data folder, open the Quarter 1 Sales.xlsx file.

    b. In the **Name Box** drop-down list, select **Quarter1**.

    c. Scroll down and observe that the range **B5:G95** is selected.

    d. Scroll up, select cell **I7** and enter *=DSUM(Quarter1,G5,I2:N3)* to determine the total sales for the month entered in cell **J3.**

    e. Observe that the total sales for the entire quarter is displayed in cell **I7.**

    f. Select cell **J7** and enter *=DAVERAGE(Quarter1,G5,I2:N3)* to determine the average sales for the month entered in the cell **J3.**

    g. Observe that the average sales for all the months in Quarter 1 is displayed in cell **J7.**

    h. Select cell **J3** and enter *Jan* to view the total and average sales of January in the cells **I7** and **J7** respectively.

Date	Month
	Jan

Sum	Average
78733	2539.7742

2. Display the report for the days when the sales for the company was less than 1000 in all the three regions.

    a. Select any cell in the table.

b. On the **Data** tab, in the **Sort & Filter** group, click **Advanced.**

c. In the **Advanced Filter** dialog box, in the **List range** text box, observe that the range is displayed as **$B$5:$G$95.**

d. In the **Criteria range** text box, select the existing text and type **$I$12:$N$13** and click **OK.**

e. Observe that the report displays only those days on which the sales for all the three regions were less than $1000.

Date	Month	United States	Canada	International	Total
1-Jan	Jan	514	314	606	1434
2-Jan	Jan	892	984	554	2430
5-Jan	Jan	826	553	607	1986
7-Jan	Jan	889	591	519	1999
10-Jan	Jan	539	574	577	1690
12-Jan	Jan	517	965	590	2072
16-Jan	Jan	595	933	654	2182
19-Jan	Jan	578	764	507	1849
20-Jan	Jan	576	529	587	1692
21-Jan	Jan	507	700	554	1761
24-Jan	Jan	885	619	555	2059
28-Jan	Jan	619	898	538	2055
5-Feb	Feb	383	496	801	1680
12-Feb	Feb	234	32	493	759
19-Feb	Feb	227	668	658	1553
26-Feb	Feb	302	503	990	1795
19-Mar	Mar	897	230	776	1903

f. On the **Data** tab, in the **Sort & Filter** group, click **Clear** to display the report for all the days.

3. Display the report for the days when sales for the company was less than $500 in any one of the region at a different location on the worksheet.

a. If necessary, select any cell in the table.

b. On the **Data** tab, in the **Sort & Filter** group, click **Advanced.**

c. In the **Advanced Filter** dialog box, in the **List range** text box, observe that the range is displayed as **$B$5:$G$95.**

d. In the **Criteria range** text box, select the text and type **$I$19:$N$22**

e. Select **Copy to another location** and click **OK.**

f. Scroll down to view the report.

g. Observe that the report displays only those days on which the sales for any one of the regions was less than $500.

h. Save the file as **My Quarter 1 Sales** and close it.

Lesson 2 Follow-up

In this lesson, you organized data in worksheets using enhanced tables and table formats. Organizing data and performing meaningful functions will enable you to get the output that you require.

1. **In your opinion, what are the various types of data that can be represented best using tables?**

2. **What do you think are some of the factors that influence the choice of a table style?**

3 Presenting Data Using Charts

Lesson Time: 45 minutes

Lesson Objectives:

In this lesson, you will create and modify charts.

You will:

- Create a chart.
- Modify charts.
- Format charts.

Introduction

In the previous lesson, you organized data in tables and worksheet data ranges. You can now use the data to build charts that display the information in a more visually effective manner. In this lesson, you will create and modify charts to graphically display data.

Even after organizing and structuring information, you may find it difficult to perform a detailed analysis of data, especially if the data set is large and complex. Microsoft® Office Excel® 2010 includes several features that allow you to present data in graphical and other logical forms. Using these features will also help you to make informed decisions.

TOPIC A
Create a Chart

In this lesson, you will present data using charts. The first step is to create the basic structure for a chart from the worksheet data. In this topic, you will create a chart.

Sometimes when you look at a large amount of data, the rows of data may seem endless. This complicated display of data makes it difficult to draw any meaningful conclusions. When you use a chart, however, you can consolidate data into a visual format that is easily understandable. By looking at the information graphically, you can quickly compare the data and assimilate information you would not have noticed otherwise.

Charts

Definition:

A *chart* is a visual representation of data from a worksheet or Excel table that displays the relationship between the different sections of data. Each set of values that is represented in the chart is called a chart *data series*. Charts include a chart title — a legend that explains what the different colors represent — a scale or values on the vertical axis, and a category on the horizontal axis. There are different chart types, such as pie, bar, and column charts. You can choose the chart type that best represents the data you want to display. A chart can be embedded as a graphic object on a worksheet page, or can be displayed on a dedicated chart sheet that contains only the chart and its associated chart tools and commands. Charts and their worksheet data are linked.

Example:

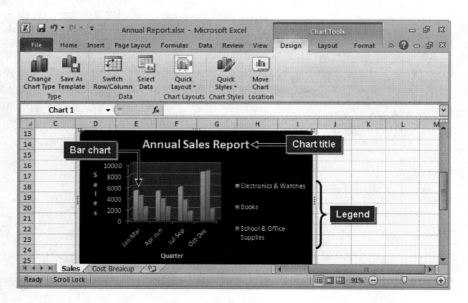

Figure 3-1: *A chart displays the relationship between different sections of data.*

Improvements to Charting Limits

Prior versions of Excel had hard limits on the number of data points in a data series. Scientific applications often require analyzing large sets of data points and, therefore, may result in memory errors if the number of data points exceeds this limit. In Excel 2010, the number of data points you can include in a chart data series is limited only by the available memory.

Types of Charts

Excel 2010 allows you to choose different chart types and subtypes for representing data.

Chart Type	*Description*
Column	Column charts are used to compare values across categories.

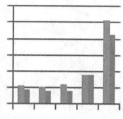

Line	Line charts are used to display trends over time.

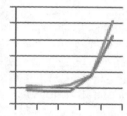

Pie	Pie charts are used to display the contribution of each value to a total. You can use a pie chart when values can be added together or when you have only one data series and all values are positive.

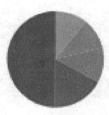

Bar	Bar charts are used for comparing multiple values.

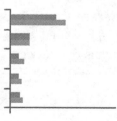

Area	Area charts are used to emphasize differences between several sets of data over a period of time.

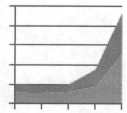

Chart Type	Description
XY (Scatter)	Scatter charts are used to compare pairs of values. You can use a scatter chart when the values being charted are not in X-axis order or when they represent separate measurements.

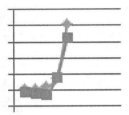

Other chart types	In addition to the major chart types, there are several specialized types:

- A stock chart, sometimes called High-Low-Close-Open, is a specialized chart type for the financial industry that displays high values, low values, closing values, opening values, and trading volume for stocks and other financial products.

- A surface chart compares trends in values across two dimensions in a continuous curve. You can use it to analyze the optimum combination of different sets of values. A surface chart must contain at least two data series.

- Doughnut charts, like pie charts, enable you to compare parts of multiple data series to the whole of each data series. However, doughnut charts can include multiple data series that display as concentric rings.

- A bubble chart is a variation on a scatter chart that compares sets of three values. The first two values determine the placement of the bubbles, while the third value determines the size of each bubble marker.

- Radar charts display changes in values relative to a center point. Use a radar chart when the data categories do not compare directly to each other, or when you want to show aggregate values.

 See the Excel Help topic "Available chart types" for more detail on chart types and subtypes.

Data Specifications for Different Chart Types

Usually, you can create a chart in Excel by plotting the data displayed as rows and columns. You can hide the rows and columns of data that you will not require. However, some chart types, such as Radar, Bubble, and Scatter charts, require specific data arrangements.

Chart Insertion Methods

If you know the type of chart you want to insert, you can use the chart type galleries in the **Charts** group on the **Insert** tab. You can also use the **Insert Chart** dialog box to choose from the available chart types. This dialog box also enables you to set a particular chart type as the default and manage your chart templates, which are built-in and formatted chart layouts that can be saved and re-used as the basis for other charts. Pressing **F11** will help you to create a chart with the default type and format on a new, dedicated chart sheet.

How to Create a Chart

Procedure Reference: Create a Chart

To create a chart based on worksheet data:

1. If necessary, arrange the worksheet or table data according to the chart to be created.

2. Select the desired data.

 When you select a single cell with data, all the adjacent cells with data around the selected cell will automatically be selected for chart creation when you insert the chart.

3. Insert the chart.
   - On the **Insert** tab, in the **Charts** group, click the button for the desired chart gallery, and select the desired chart subtype from the gallery.
   - Or, create a chart using the **Insert Chart** dialog box.
     a. On the **Insert** tab, in the **Charts** group, either click the **Dialog Box Launcher** button, or open any chart gallery and select **All Chart Types.**
     b. In the left pane, select a chart type.
     c. In the right pane, select a chart subtype and click **OK.**
   - Or, press **F11** to create the chart on a dedicated chart sheet.

Adding Data to an Existing Chart

After you create a chart, you can add an additional data series to the chart rather than completely re-creating it.

ACTIVITY 3-1
Creating Charts

Data Files:

Annual Report.xlsx

Scenario:

You are asked to present a report on the sales of various categories of goods sold by OGC Stores in the last fiscal at the annual board meeting. Your manager has requested that you create the report in a way that the board members will be able to clearly see the relationship between the different sections of data. You have decided to use a column chart to display the monthly sales of different category of goods and a line chart to display the sales of books for different months. Also, the finance manager has asked you to add another sheet in the same workbook that shows the breakup of overall capital.

1. Create a 3-D Column chart from the data to compare the monthly sales of products.

   a. From the C:\084577Data\Presenting Data Using Charts folder, open the Annual Report.xlsx file.

   b. On the **Sales** worksheet, select any cell in the first table.

   c. On the **Insert** tab, in the **Charts** group, click the **Column** drop-down.

   d. In the displayed gallery, in the **3-D Column** section, select the first option to create a **3–D Clustered Column** chart.

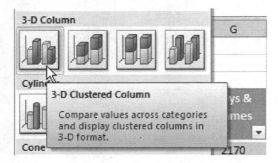

   e. Observe that the chart is created and the **Chart Tools Design** contextual tab appears because the chart is selected.

f.   Click the chart border and drag the chart to the right of the first table.

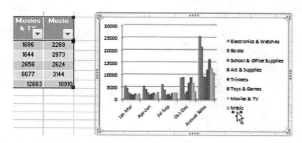

2.   Create a Line chart to display the trend in the sales of books.

a.   Select any cell in the second table.

b.   On the **Insert** tab, in the **Charts** group, in the lower-right corner, click the **Create Chart** dialog box launcher.

c.   In the **Insert Chart** dialog box, in the left pane, select **Line** and, in the right pane, in the **Line** section, select the left-most line chart and click **OK.**

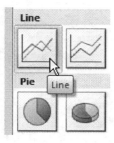

d.   Click the chart border and drag the chart to the right of the second table.

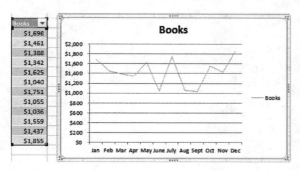

3.   Create a 3-D Pie chart to display the cost breakup for year 2010.

a.   On the **Cost Breakup** worksheet, select the ranges **A4:A11** and **D4:D11.**

b.   On the **Insert** tab, in the **Charts** group, click the **Pie** drop-down.

c. In the displayed gallery, in the **3-D Pie** section, select **Pie in 3-D,** the left-most option.

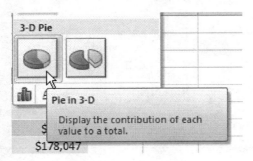

d. Click the chart border and drag the chart to the right of the **2010 Breakup** column.

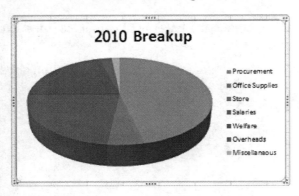

e. Save the file as *My Annual Report*

TOPIC B
Modify Charts

In the previous topic, you inserted a chart. Once you have created a basic chart, you can modify its structure in various ways to suit your needs. In this topic, you will modify charts.

The default format of a chart item may or may not convey the correct meaning the data in your chart represents. Your chart won't be very useful if the chart items that explain the data are misleading or difficult to understand. Instead, you can format each chart item to appear exactly as required, to meet your business needs.

Chart Elements

You can choose from a variety of chart elements to include in a chart. Your choice will, however, depend upon the chart type and its associated elements.

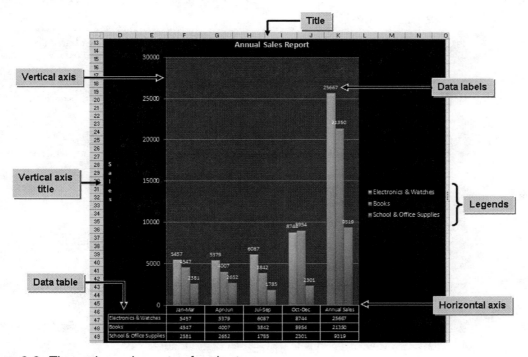

Figure 3-2: *The various elements of a chart.*

Chart Element	Purpose
Chart title	Describes what the overall chart represents.
Category (X) axis title	Describes what the X axis represents.
Value (Y) axis title	Describes what the Y axis represents.
Axes	The reference lines that are drawn on a graph for measuring the values. In charts displaying multiple data series, the X axis shows the data series in each category, and the Y axis shows how the data is measured (amount, time, and others).

Chart Element	Purpose
Gridlines	For charts with axes, each of the X and Y axes can display both major and minor gridlines.
Legend	Indicates what color or symbol represents which particular data series.
Data labels	Indicates the numeric value, the percentage, or the name of a single data point.
Data table	Displays the worksheet data that the chart is based on in a table below the chart.

Chart Tools Contextual Tabs

The **Chart Tools** contextual tabs that appear when you select a chart enable you to manipulate the appearance and layout of the chart.

Contextual Tab	Description
Design	Provides options to modify the style, layout, data source, and type of chart. The groups on the tab are: • **Type**: Provides options to change the type of chart and to save as a template. • **Data**: Provides options to switch between the row and column data, as well as to edit the data source. • **Chart Layouts**: Provides options to modify the layout of the chart. • **Chart Styles**: Provides options to change the appearance of the chart to one of the preset styles in the Quick Styles gallery. • **Location**: Provides options to move the chart to another worksheet or to another chart.
Layout	Provides options for further customizing chart elements. The groups on the tab are: • **Current Selection**: Allows a chart element to be selected and formatted. • **Insert**: Allows for inserting pictures, shapes, and text boxes. • **Labels**: Provides options to manage labels on various locations of a chart. • **Axes**: Provides options to manage the formatting of axes and gridlines. • **Background**: Provides options to modify the background elements of a chart. • **Analysis**: Provides options to add elements for aiding analysis. • **Properties**: Provides an option to specify a chart name.
Format	Provides options to format the chart and chart elements. The tab consists of these button groups: • **Current Selection**: Allows a chart element to be selected and formatted. • **Shape Styles**: Provides options to modify the color, style, and effects applied to a shape. • **WordArt Styles**: Provides options to preview **WordArt** styles and modify the fill color, line color, and effects. **WordArt** is a method for treating text as a graphic object. • **Arrange**: Provides options to arrange, align, and rotate the shapes, **WordArt**, or text boxes. • **Size**: Provides options to modify the width and height of the selected graphical object.

How to Modify Charts

Procedure Reference: Change a Chart Type

To change a chart type:

1. Select the chart.
2. On the **Chart Tools Design** contextual tab, in the **Type** group, click **Change Chart Type.**
3. In the **Change Chart Type** dialog box, select a chart type and subtype and click **OK.**

Changing the Type of an Existing Data Series

You can also select any data series and change its type independently of the rest of the data series.

Procedure Reference: Resize a Chart

To resize a chart:

1. In an Excel workbook containing a chart, select the chart.
2. Resize the chart.
   - Drag the border of the chart to resize the chart without maintaining its scale.
   - Hold **Shift** as you drag the border of the chart to resize the chart while maintaining its scale.
   - On the **Chart Tools Format** contextual tab, in the **Size** group, in the **Shape Height** and **Shape Width** spin boxes, type or select the desired height and width of the chart to resize the chart to a fixed size.

Procedure Reference: Move a Chart Between Sheets

To move a chart from one sheet to another:

1. Select the chart.
2. On the **Ribbon**, select the **Chart Tools Design** contextual tab.
3. In the **Location** group, click **Move Chart** to display the **Move Chart** dialog box.
4. Move the chart.
   - To move the chart to another worksheet, select **Object In**, select the sheet from the drop-down list, and click **OK.** If needed, reposition the chart on the worksheet.
   - To move the chart to a chart sheet, select **New Sheet**, type the sheet name, and click **OK.**

Procedure Reference: Add or Remove Chart Elements

To add or remove chart elements:

1. Click anywhere inside an Excel chart to select it.
2. On the **Ribbon**, select the **Chart Tools Layout** contextual tab.
3. To add a chart title, in the **Labels** group, click **Chart Title** and choose **Above Chart** or **Centered Overlay Title.**

4. For a chart that has an axis, use the **Axis Titles** button in the **Labels** group to add axis titles.

   - To add a horizontal axis title, click **Axis Titles** and choose **Primary Horizontal Axis Title→Title Below Axis.**

   - Or, to add a vertical axis title, click **Axis Titles**, choose **Primary Vertical Axis Title**, and then choose **Rotated Title**, **Vertical Title**, or **Horizontal Title.**

5. To add a legend to the chart, in the **Labels** group, click **Legend** and choose the desired option. You can display the legend at the top, bottom, left, or right of the chart, or overlay the legend on the left or right side of the chart.

6. To add data labels, in the **Labels** group, click **Data Labels** and select the desired option. You can display the data labels centered on the data points inside or outside the end of the data points, or inside the base of the data points.

7. If desired, click **Data Labels** and select **More Data Label** options to set other label options.

8. To add a data table, in the **Labels** group, click **Data Table** and then choose **Show Data Table** or **Show Data Table With Legend Keys.**

9. To change the chart scale, in the **Axes** group, click **Axes** and choose **Primary Horizontal Axis** or **Primary Vertical Axis.** The choices available will vary depending upon your chart type and orientation.

   - For the vertical axis, you can show the default values, or show the scale in thousands, millions, billions, or logarithmically.

   - Or, for the horizontal axis, you can show the default axis (labels from left to right), the axis with no label, or display the axis with labels from right to left.

10. To add gridlines, in the **Axes** group, click **Gridlines**, choose **Primary Horizontal Gridlines** or **Primary Vertical Gridlines**, and choose the appropriate option. You can display major or minor gridlines or both.

11. Remove chart elements as needed.

    - Select the chart element and press **Delete**, or right-click it and choose **Delete**.

    - Or, click the element's button in the **Labels** group and choose **None.**

 When you click **Legend** and select **None** in the Labels group, the entire legend group is removed. To remove a single legend item, select the individual item and delete it.

ACTIVITY 3-2
Changing a Chart Type

Before You Begin:

My Annual Report.xlsx is open and the 3–D pie chart on the Cost Breakup worksheet is displayed.

Scenario:

After reviewing the annual report, your manager feels that the 3–D pie chart displaying the cost breakup could be further enhanced using a 3–D exploded pie chart, which will display all components of the cost breakup distinctly. While changing the chart type, you also decide to display the percentage values for each component and adjust the font for better visibility.

1. Change the 3–D pie chart on the Cost Breakup worksheet to exploded 3–D pie chart.

   a. On the **Chart Tools Design** contextual tab, in the **Type** group, click **Change Chart Type.**

   b. In the **Change Chart Type** dialog box, in the right pane, scroll down and from the **Pie** section, select **Exploded pie in 3–D**, which is the fifth option from left and click **OK.**

   c. Observe that the pie chart changes to exploded view.

   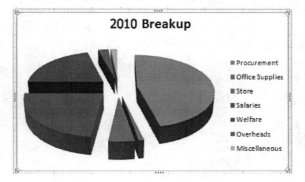

2. Apply a Chart Style to the chart.

   a. In the **Chart Tools Design** contextual tab, from the **Chart Styles** group, click the **More** button.

b. In the gallery, from the fifth row, select the second style from left to apply **Style 34** to the pie chart.

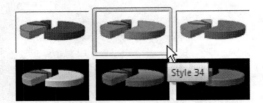

c. On the **Chart Tools Layout** tab, in the **Labels** group, click the **Data Labels** drop-down and select **More Data Label Options.**

d. In the **Format Data Labels** dialog box, on the **Label Options** tab, in the **Label Contains** section, uncheck **Value** and select **Percentage** and click **Close.**

e. Observe that the pie chart displays the percentage values.

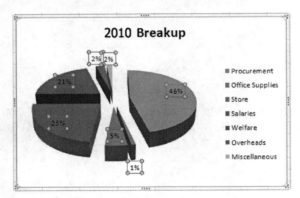

f. Right-click the percentage value corresponding to **Procurement** and choose **Font.**

g. In the **Font** dialog box, on the **Font** tab, in the **Size** spin box, triple-click and type *15*

h. In the **Font style** drop-down, select **Bold** and click **OK.**

i. Observe that the percentage values are displayed with a font size of 15 and are bold formatted.

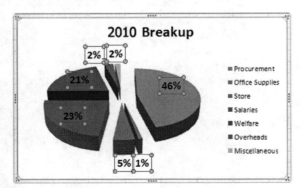

j. Save the file.

ACTIVITY 3-3
Modifying a Chart

Before You Begin:

My Annual Report.xlsx is open and the column chart on the Sales worksheet is displayed.

Scenario:

You have just created charts for different sets of data that you want to present to the board members of your company. After making certain modifications to them, you feel that a particular column chart could be moved to a new sheet for better representation. You also want to add axes titles to the chart.

1. Move the column chart to a chart sheet and title the sheet as "Annual Sales."

    a. On the **Sales** sheet, select the column chart.

    b. On the **Chart Tools Design** contextual tab, in the **Location** group, click **Move Chart.**

    c. In the **Move Chart** dialog box, select the **New sheet** option, and in the **New sheet** text box, type *Annual Sales* and click **OK.**

    d. Observe that the column chart gets displayed in a new sheet titled **Annual Sales.**

2. Add the title Annual Sales Report to the column chart.

    a. On the **Chart Tools Layout** contextual tab, in the **Labels** group, click **Chart Title** and choose **Above Chart.**

    b. In the **Formula** bar, enter *Annual Sales Report*

    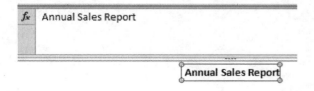

3. On the column chart, add the horizontal and vertical axes titles.

    a. In the **Labels** group, click **Axis Titles** and choose **Primary Horizontal Axis Title→ Title Below Axis.**

b. Scroll down to view the title of the horizontal axis.

c. In the **Formula** bar, enter *Quarter*

d. In the **Labels** group, click **Axis Titles** and choose **Primary Vertical Axis Title→ Vertical Title.**

e. In the **Formula** bar, enter *Sales*

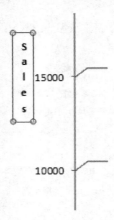

f. Save the file.

TOPIC C
Format Charts

In the previous topic, you modified structural elements of a chart. You now have the ability to change the appearance of any or all of the chart elements that you want to include. In this topic, you will format charts.

You may create a chart and later decide that you would like to change the style and the layout of the chart to better represent your data. There are many styles and layouts to choose from to format your chart and represent the data in the best way possible.

Chart Styles and Formatting Options

After creating a chart, you can change the appearance of individual chart elements by using options on the **Chart Tools Format** contextual tab. For example, you can change the color of chart columns or the chart background. However, instead of manually formatting individual chart elements, you can choose predefined styles to quickly change the appearance of the entire chart. The styles available are based on the type of chart you have created.

Chart Layouts

You can add or remove individual chart elements such as the title or legend. Or, you can implement a standard set of chart elements by applying one of the predefined chart layouts from the **Chart Layouts** group on the **Chart Tools Design** contextual tab. You can then use the options on the **Chart Tools Layout** contextual tab to customize the appearance of individual chart elements.

How to Format Charts

Procedure Reference: Format Charts

To format charts or chart elements:

1. On the worksheet, select the chart to be formatted.
2. To apply a style, select the **Chart Tools Design** contextual tab and, in the **Chart Styles** group, select the desired chart style.
3. To apply a layout, select the **Chart Tools Design** contextual tab and, in the **Chart Layouts** group, select the desired chart layout.
4. Modify the labels or properties of individual chart elements.
   a. Select the chart element.
   b. Select the **Chart Tools Layout** contextual tab.
   c. In the **Labels** group, select the chart element whose label you want to modify, and from the drop-down menu, choose the options to insert, delete, or modify the labels.
5. Format individual chart elements.
   a. Select the chart element.
   b. Select the **Chart Tools Format** contextual tab.
   c. In the **Shape Styles** group, select the desired shape style, shape fill, shape outline, and shape effect or in the **WordArt Styles** group, select the desired WordArt style, text fill, text outline, and text effect.

Enhancements to User Interface

The chart formatting options in Excel 2010 can be activated by double-clicking the chart element to be formatted. This allows you to select the element to be formatted right from the chart itself, without navigating through the options on the ribbon.

ACTIVITY 3-4
Formatting a Chart

Before You Begin:

My Annual Report.xlsx is open with the line chart on the Sales worksheet displayed.

Scenario:

After creating a line chart to represent the sales trend of books, you would like to format the chart to enhance its presentation by having it in a different color style. You would also like to emphasize the horizontal axis of the chart.

1. Apply a chart style to the line chart.

   a. Select the line chart.

   b. On the **Chart Tools Design** contextual tab, in the **Chart Styles** group, click the **More** button.

   c. In the gallery, in the fifth row, select **Style 33,** the first option from left.

2. Change the chart layout.

   a. In the **Chart Layouts** group, click the **More** button.

   b. In the gallery, in the third row, click the first layout from left to apply **Layout 7** to the chart.

   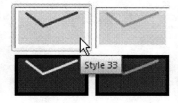

   c. On the **Sales** worksheet, in the chart corresponding to the book sales, add the horizontal and vertical axis titles as *Month* and *Sales* respectively.

3. Format the border of the chart.

   a. Select the **Chart Tools Format** contextual tab.

   b. In the **Shape Styles** group, click the **Shape Effects** drop-down and select **Glow**.

c. In the gallery, in the **Glow Variations** section, in the fourth row, select the second option from left to apply the **Olive Green, 18 pt glow, Accent color 6** effect to the chart.

d. Observe that the selected shape effect is applied to the line chart.

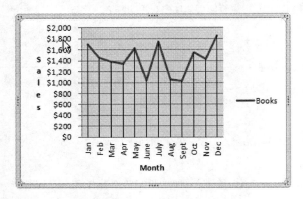

e. Save the file and close it.

Lesson 3 Follow-up

In this lesson, you displayed data using charts. Charts enable you to view a large amount of data at a glance and help you to draw relevant conclusions quickly.

1. **In your opinion, what are the advantages of representing information through charts?**

2. **What types of charts are you familiar with? Do you think one particular type of chart is better than the rest? Why?**

4 | Analyzing Data Using PivotTables, Slicers, and PivotCharts

Lesson Time: 1 hour(s), 15 minutes

Lesson Objectives:

In this lesson, you will analyze data using PivotTables, Slicers, and PivotCharts.

You will:

- Create a PivotTable report.
- Use Slicers for filtering data.
- Analyze data using PivotCharts.

Introduction

In the previous lesson, you inserted tables and charts into your documents. PivotTables and PivotCharts take chart and table functionality one step further and enable you to selectively analyze the data in your worksheet in sophisticated and interactive ways. In this lesson, you will create PivotTables and PivotCharts and use their associated tools to analyze data.

When you have a large number of data to be analyzed, it may not be easy for you to compare the required elements manually. Microsoft® Office Excel® 2010 provides powerful PivotChart and PivotTable features that enable you to view only those data elements that you wish to analyze. Also, Excel 2010 includes Slicers that allow you to filter complex PivotTable and PivotChart data.

TOPIC A

Create a PivotTable Report

In this lesson, you will create PivotTables and PivotCharts to analyze data. Creating a PivotTable report by itself will help you understand the structure of the report. In this topic, you will create a PivotTable.

Performing manual comparisons of large amounts of data is difficult. A PivotTable can quickly combine and compare data for you to perform analysis on large amounts of data. PivotTable reports allow you to filter all unnecessary data that makes analyzing large worksheet data much easier.

PivotTable

Definition:

A *PivotTable* report is an interactive worksheet table that you can use to summarize and analyze large amounts of worksheet data quickly. It displays the selected worksheet data in a matrix format with specialized functionality that enables you to see new data relationships; summarize, group, and format selected portions of the data; pivot the data between columns and rows; and create concise customized output. You can create a PivotTable report from source data in an Excel workbook or from an external data source. To specify which portion of the source data to use in a PivotTable report, you have to first identify the required fields and items. Fields are categories of data, usually columns, and items are subcategories in a field.

Example:

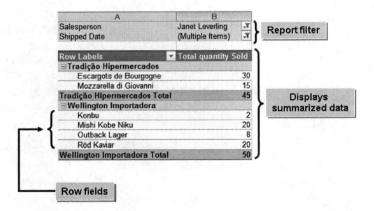

Source data

Figure 4-1: *A PivotTable report summarizes large amounts of worksheet data in a simpler format.*

Types of PivotTable Fields

There are four types of PivotTable fields: page, row, column, and data fields. Page, row, and column fields usually contain a limited set of text values. Data fields usually contain numeric data.

The PivotTable Field List Pane

The **PivotTable Field List** pane is displayed when you select a **PivotTable** report. The pane includes drop zones, wherein you can drag and drop fields in order to reorient and rearrange data and calculated values in multiple formats quickly. It also includes the **Report Filter** drop zone for fields that need to be eliminated from PivotTable reports. You can make informed decisions more efficiently by manipulating the **PivotTable** report results interactively.

Hiding or Displaying the PivotTable Field List Pane

The PivotTable Field List pane can be displayed by right-clicking the PivotTable and choosing **Show Field List.**

The Value Field Settings Dialog Box

Using the **Value Field Settings** dialog box, you can display or hide subtotals for individual column and row fields, display or hide column and row grand totals for the entire report, and calculate the subtotals and grand totals with or without filtered items. The field settings can be customized and given a name so that you can reuse them for specific summary calculations.

PivotTable Functions

Several functions are available for use while creating formulas to work with PivotTable data.

Function	*Result*
Difference From	Displays the data as a difference of the value for the specified base field and the base item. The base field is the field that is being used for filtering the PivotTable. The item within the base field for which data is displayed is known as the base item.
% Of	Displays the data as a percentage of the value for the specified base field and base item. The base field and base item provide the data used in the custom calculation.
% Difference From	Displays the data as the difference of the value for the specified base field and the base item, but it also displays the difference as a percentage of the base data. The base field and base item provide the data used in the custom calculation.
Running Total In	Displays the data for successive items as a running total. You must select the field for which you want to show the items in a running total.
% Of Row	Displays the data in each row as a percentage of the total for each row. When the data in the PivotTables is represented in a graphical format through PivotChart reports, the % Of Row function displays the data as a percentage of the total for the category.
% Of Column	Displays the data in each column as a percentage of the total for each column. In a PivotChart report, it displays the data as a percentage of the total for the series.

Function	Result
% Of Total	Displays the data in the data area as a percentage of the grand total of all the data in the report. In a PivotChart report, it displays the data as a percentage of the total of all data points.
Index	Displays the data by using the following calculation: ((Value in cell) x (Grand Total of Grand Totals)) / ((Grand Row Total) x (Grand Column Total))

Additional PivotTable Functions

Excel 2010 also includes a **Show Values As** context menu, which displays additional calculations that can be applied to fields in a PivotTable. There are six calculation options on this menu, including **% of Parent Row Total, % of Parent Column Total, % of Parent Total, % Running Total In, Rank Smallest to Largest,** and **Rank Largest to Smallest.** These functions are new to Excel 2010. Additionally, you can use the **What-If-Analysis** feature to modify values in PivotTable cells.

PowerPivot

PowerPivot is an Excel 2010 add-in that allows users to import data from various sources and analyze them using PivotTables. It is used for importing data from applications other than Excel and for processing such data using Excel tools. Using PowerPivot you can integrate data from multiple sources and manipulate large data sets with ease.

 Microsoft PowerPivot is available as a free download for Excel 2010 users at **http://www.powerpivot.com/download.aspx**.

How to Create a PivotTable Report
Procedure Reference: Create a PivotTable Report

To create a PivotTable report from Excel worksheet data:

1. In the worksheet, select a cell in the data range you want to use as the source data.
2. On the **Insert** tab, in the **Tables** group, click **PivotTable.**
3. In the **Create PivotTable** dialog box, specify the data range, choose whether you want the PivotTable on a new sheet or an existing sheet, and then click **OK.**

4. Select the layout of the fields in the PivotTable:

   a. If necessary, click the drop-drop button at the top of the **PivotTable Field List** pane and select a report layout.

   b. If necessary, in the **Choose fields to add to report** list box, check or uncheck the check boxes to select fields for the PivotTable report.

   c. To use a field in a specific area of the report, from the **Choose fields to add to report** list box, drag the desired fields to the **Report Filter, Column Labels, Row Labels**, or **Values** drop zone.

   d. If desired, check **Defer Layout Update** if you want to use the **Update** button to manually update the PivotTable report.

   e. To move a field to a different area, drag the field, or click the field's drop-down and make the appropriate selection.

5. Group fields in the PivotTable report.

   a. In the worksheet, in the PivotTable report, select the desired fields.

   b. Group the fields.

      ● On the **Ribbon**, on the **PivotTable Tools Options** contextual tab, in the **Group** group, click **Group Selection.**

      ● Or, right-click the selected fields and choose **Group.**

   c. Select the group heading, and in the **Formula** bar text box, type the desired group name.

   d. If desired, select and group other fields in the report.

   e. To expand or collapse the group, click the (+) button or click the (-) button.

Manual vs. Automatic Updating

The layout of a PivotTable is updated automatically as soon as the changes are made to the drop zones in the **PivotTable Field List** pane. Users can check the **Defer Layout Option** at the bottom of the **PivotTable Field List** pane to prevent automatic updates to the PivotTable. To manually update the PivotTable, users need to click the **Update** button.

Procedure Reference: Customize the Calculations in a PivotTable

To customize the calculations in a PivotTable:

1. If necessary, display the **PivotTable Field List** pane.

   a. Select the PivotTable report.

   b. If the **PivotTable Field List** pane does not appear, on the **PivotTable Tools Options** contextual tab, in the **Show/Hide** group, click the **Field List** button.

2. Display the **Value Field Settings** dialog box.

   ● In the **PivotTable Field List** pane, in the **Values** list box, click the drop-down or the desired field and choose **Value Field Settings.**

   ● Or, in the worksheet, in the PivotTable report, right-click a cell that is related to the values in the **PivotTable Field List** pane, and choose **Value Field Settings.**

3. Customize calculations using the **Value Field Settings** dialog box.

   a. If necessary, in the **Custom Name** text box, type the desired name to name the column.

   b. On the **Summarize By** tab, in the list box, select the desired calculations.

   c. To format the field, click **Number Format**, select a format, and click **OK.**

4. Click **OK** to customize the calculation of the column.

5. If necessary, repeat steps 2, 3 and 4 to customize the calculation of other columns.

Procedure Reference: Change Field Settings for Non-Value Fields

To change field settings for non-value fields:

1. Display the **PivotTable Field List** pane.

2. Display the **Field Settings** dialog box.

   - In the **PivotTable Field List** pane, in the **Column Labels**, **Report Filter**, or **Row Labels** drop box, click the drop-down list for the desired field and choose **Field Settings.**

   - Or, in the worksheet, in the PivotTable report, right-click a cell that is considered to be a non-value field, and choose **Field Settings.**

3. Change the field settings as per your requirement.

   - If necessary, in the **Custom Name** text box, type the desired name to change the name of the field.

   - If necessary, on the **Subtotals & Filters** tab, in the **Subtotals** section, select the desired option, **Automatic**, **None**, or **Custom**, to add subtotals to the groups in the PivotTable report.

   - If necessary, in the **Select one or more functions** list box, select the desired functions.

   - If necessary, in the **Filter** section, check **Include New Items In Manual Filter.**

   - If necessary, select the **Layout & Print** tab and select the desired options.

4. Click **OK.**

Procedure Reference: Sort or Filter a PivotTable Report

To sort or filter a PivotTable report:

1. Use the method of your choice to sort the report.

   - In the worksheet, in the PivotTable, click the **Column Labels** or **Row Labels** filter drop-down list and select the desired sort option.

   - Or, in the **Choose fields to add to report** list box, place the mouse pointer over the desired field name, click the displayed arrow, and select the desired sort option.

2. Use the method of your choice to filter the report.

   - In the **Choose fields to add to report** list box, place the mouse pointer over the desired field name, click the displayed arrow, and select the desired filter option.

   - In the worksheet, in the PivotTable, click the **(All)** filter drop-down list and select the desired filter option.

 The **Report Filter** drop-down list appears only for those fields that have already been dragged from the **Choose fields to add to report** list box to the **Report Filter** list box in the **PivotTable Field List** pane.

Procedure Reference: Modify the PivotTable Report

To modify the PivotTable report:

1. Select the PivotTable.

2. Select the **PivotTable Tools Design** contextual tab.

3. In the **Layout** group, select the desired options from the **Grand Totals**, **Subtotals**, **Report Layout**, and **Blank Rows** drop-down lists.

4. Select formatting options in the **PivotTable Style Options** and **PivotTable Styles** groups.

5. Select the **PivotTable Tools Options** contextual tab.

6. In the **Show/Hide** group, click **+/-** button to display or hide the expand (**+**) or collapse (**-**) button in front of the group headers.

7. In the **Show/Hide** group, click **Field Headers** to display or hide the field headers in the PivotTable report.

8. If desired, print the report.

ACTIVITY 4-1
Creating a PivotTable

Data Files:

Shipping.xlsx

Scenario:

The Shipping workbook contains a large volume of information about the products that were shipped by Everything For Coffee LLC in the past several months. Your manager has requested a report to review the total quantity of the products that Anne sold in the month of January, sorted by company. Since you are confident that your manager might have a similar request for information on other salespersons as well, you decide to create a PivotTable report to easily extract the information without constantly having to rearrange the data by sorting and re-creating formulas.

1. Create a PivotTable report of sales by each salesperson and shipped date.

    a. From the C:\084577Data\Analyzing Data Using PivotTables, Slicers, and PivotCharts folder, open the Shipping.xlsx file.

    b. On the **Insert** tab, in the **Tables** group, click the **PivotTable** drop-down and choose **PivotTable.**

    c. In the **Create PivotTable** dialog box, verify that **Select a table or range** and **New Worksheet** are selected and then click **OK** to create the PivotTable.

    d. In the **PivotTable Field List** pane, in the **Choose fields to add to report** list box, check **Salesperson, Shipped Date, Product Name**, and **Quantity** to show these items on the PivotTable report.

e. Observe that Excel automatically determines the most appropriate field from what has been checked in the list to place in the **Values** list box.

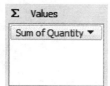

---

2. Change the column label in the PivotTable report to "Total Quantity Sold" by using the Values Field Settings dialog box.

   a. In the **PivotTable Field List** pane, in the **Drag fields between areas below** section, in the **Values** list box, click the **Sum of Quantity** drop-down arrow and select **Value Field Settings.**

   b. In the **Value Field Settings** dialog box, on the **Summarize Values By** tab, in the **Summarize value field by** list, verify that **Sum** is selected by default and click **Number Format.**

   c. In the **Format Cells** dialog box, in the **Category** list box, verify that **General** is selected and click **OK.**

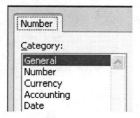

   d. In the **Value Field Settings** dialog box, in the **Custom Name** text box, replace the default text with *Total Quantity Sold* and click **OK.**

   e. Verify that the **PivotTable Report** displays the new label as **Total Quantity Sold.**

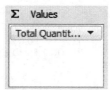

---

3. Create a filter to group the PivotTable by Salesperson and then display products that Anne Dodsworth sold.

   a. In the **PivotTable Field List** pane, from the **Choose fields to add to report** list box, drag the **Salesperson** field to the **Report Filter** box.

b.   On the worksheet, from the **Salesperson** filter drop-down list, select **Anne Dodsworth** and click **OK.**

c.   Observe that the products are displayed in the ascending order of the shipped date. The first three products do not have the shipping date and are therefore listed on the top.

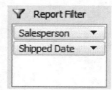

---

4.   Display products that Anne Dodsworth sold that were shipped in the month of January.

a.   From the **Choose fields to add to report** list box, drag the **Shipped Date** field to the **Report Filter** box and drop it below **Salesperson.**

b.   In the worksheet, in the **Shipped Date** filter drop-down list, check **Select Multiple Items.**

c.   In the **Shipped Date Items** list, uncheck **(All)** and check **1/1/2009** through **1/31/2009** and click **OK.**

d.   Observe that the PivotTable displays the total quantity of each product sold by Anne Dodsworth.

---

5.   In the PivotTable report, display the names of the companies to which the products were being shipped.

a.   From the **Choose fields to add to report** list box, drag **Company Name** to the **Row Labels** drop box above **Product Name.**

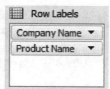

b.　Observe that the PivotTable report now shows the total quantity of products sold by Anne Dodsworth, grouped by the company name.

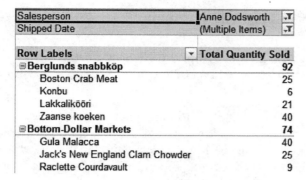

| Salesperson | Anne Dodsworth | |
| Shipped Date | (Multiple Items) | |

Row Labels	Total Quantity Sold
⊟ **Berglunds snabbköp**	**92**
Boston Crab Meat	25
Konbu	6
Lakkalikööri	21
Zaanse koeken	40
⊟ **Bottom-Dollar Markets**	**74**
Gula Malacca	40
Jack's New England Clam Chowder	25
Raclette Courdavault	9

c.　Close the **PivotTable Field List** pane.

6.　Display the subtotals in a separate row at the bottom of each group and format the Pivot-Table report.

a.　On the **PivotTable Tools Design** contextual tab, in the **Layout** group, click the **Sub-totals** drop-down and choose **Show all Subtotals at Bottom of Group.**

b.　In the **PivotTable Styles** group, click the **More** button.

c.　In the displayed gallery, in the **Medium** section, in the second row, select **Pivot Style Medium 9,** the second option from left.

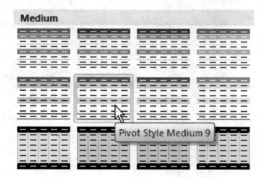

d.　In the **PivotTable Style Options** group, check **Banded Rows.**

e.　Save the file as *My Shipping*

TOPIC B
Filter Data Using Slicers

You are familiar with creating PivotTables. Excel 2010 also includes a related feature known as a Slicer that extends the filtering capabilities of PivotTables. In this topic, you will use Slicers to filter PivotTable data.

Though you can filter data in a PivotTable by using the Report Filters drop zone, it is not easy to see the current state of the PivotTable when filtering multiple items. Filtering using Slicers allows users to view the current filtering state of the PivotTables, which makes it easy to understand what exactly is shown in a filtered PivotTable report. Slicers also make it easier to apply filtering criteria to the PivotTables.

Slicers

A *Slicer* is a filtering tool that allows users to include only the required elements in the Pivot-Tables and PivotCharts. It allows users to add and remove elements from the table display so that the data can be compared and evaluated from different perspectives. Users can choose more than one Slicer for a PivotTable, if required. Slicers can be used with multiple Pivot-Tables to showcase your data consistently in a variety of scenarios. Slicers can be placed either on the same worksheet containing the PivotTable or on a different worksheet.

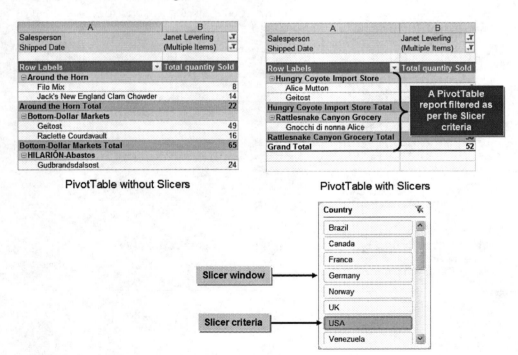

Figure 4-2: *Slicers can be used for filtering data in PivotTables.*

The Insert Slicers Dialog Box

The **Insert Slicers** dialog box allows you to select the fields for slicing PivotTable data. This dialog box can be launched from the **Insert Slicer** drop-down, which is located in the **Sort & Filter** group on the **PivotTables Tools Options** contextual tab.

How to Use Slicers in Excel

Procedure Reference: Apply Slicers to a PivotTable

To apply Slicers to a PivotTable:

1. Select the PivotTable for which you want to apply Slicers.

2. On the **PivotTable Tool Options** contextual tab, from the **Sort & Filter** group, click the **Insert Slicer** drop-down menu and choose **Insert Slicer.**

3. In the **Insert Slicers** dialog box, check the fields that you want to display in the PivotTable and click **OK.**

4. On the **Slicer** window, select the appropriate data item for which you want to display in the PivotTable.

ACTIVITY 4-2
Filtering PivotTable Data Using Slicers

Before You Begin
The file My Shipping.xlsx is open.

Scenario:
Your manager has asked you to create a report showing the sales information of each salesperson for presentation. He wants you to display the data for each salesperson grouped by country. Though you entered the data in a PivotTable format, you want to further filter it so as to keep the presentation as simple as possible. To make the presentation simple, you decide to apply Slicers to the PivotTable so that you can switch between different salespersons.

---

1. Define Slicers for your table.

    a. On the **PivotTable Tool Options** contextual tab, in the **Sort & Filter** group, click the **Insert Slicer** drop-down and choose **Insert Slicer.**

    b. In the **Insert Slicers** dialog box, check the **Country** and **Salesperson** check boxes and click **OK.**

c. Observe that two Slicer windows are placed on the worksheet.

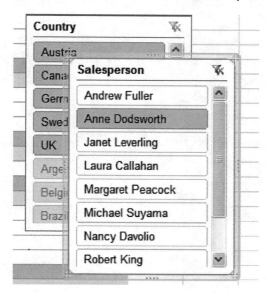

d. Reposition the Slicer windows to view the entire PivotTable.

2. View the information related to individual salespersons in a country.

a. In the **Country** Slicer window, select **Brazil** to display the information specific to the country.

b. Observe that there is no sales data available for the salesperson Anne Dodsworth in Brazil for the month of January, indicating that she has not sold anything in Brazil in January.

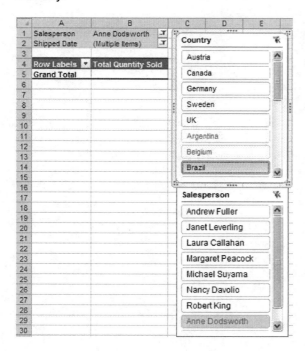

c. In the **Salesperson** Slicer window, select **Janet Leverling** to display the information specific to the salesperson.

d.   Observe that the sales data for the salesperson Janet Leverling in Brazil is displayed in the PivotTable report.

e.   If necessary, choose any other country and salesperson of your choice to view information specific to that country and salesperson.

f.   Save the file.

TOPIC C

Analyze Data Using PivotCharts

In the previous topic, you created a PivotTable report. Another approach to creating a report is to create a PivotChart along with the PivotTable report. In this topic, you will analyze data using PivotCharts.

Graphical representation of data makes data analysis a lot easier task. Though PivotTables can generate reports that are easy to understand, you may also want to show a visual representation of the data, for example, in cases where there is a trend over time, such as growth or decline on a monthly or yearly basis. In this case, you may want to focus on a particular quarter to highlight revenue growth. PivotChart reports help facilitate data analysis by graphically representing data from PivotTable reports.

PivotCharts

Definition:

A *PivotChart* is an interactive chart that graphically represents the data in a PivotTable report. When you create a PivotChart report, a PivotTable report associated with the chart is also created. A chart contains standard chart elements, although you can make changes to it by changing its type or layout.

Unlike a regular chart, however, a PivotChart is tied to its PivotTable report's contents and functionality, not to worksheet cells. A PivotChart, therefore, represents the current state of the PivotTable report, and there's no need to edit or revise the source data. In Excel 2010, you can use the shortcut menu options to change the position of fields on a PivotChart. You can also filter data you want to view by using the drop-down lists displayed on the PivotChart, or remove the displayed data by choosing the **Show/Hide Field** buttons on the **Analyze** tab.

Example:

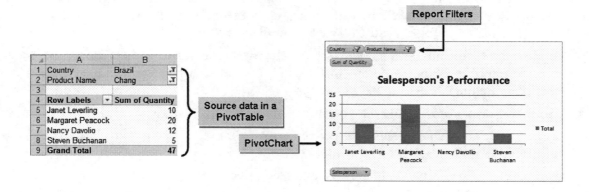

Figure 4-3: A PivotChart generated from a PivotTable.

Formatting Limitations of PivotCharts

PivotCharts can be any chart type except for XY, stock, or bubble charts. When you refresh a PivotChart report, most of the chart formatting will also refresh. However, because the chart is based on varying data in a PivotTable, chart elements that are tied to specific data series, such as trendlines and data labels, are not preserved. You might need to re-apply these chart elements.

How to Analyze Data Using PivotCharts

Procedure Reference: Create a PivotChart

To create a PivotChart:

1. In the spreadsheet, select a cell with data.
2. On the **Ribbon**, select the **Insert** tab.
3. In the **Tables** group, click the **PivotTable** drop-down list and select **PivotChart.**
4. In the **Create PivotTable with PivotChart** dialog box, specify the data range, specify the location for the PivotChart and PivotTable, and then click **OK.**
5. Use the **PivotTable Field List** pane to construct the PivotTable by selecting a table layout and adding fields. The PivotTable and PivotChart will then appear in the specified worksheet.

Procedure Reference: Analyze PivotChart Data

To analyze PivotChart data:

1. Use the **PivotTable Field List** pane to restructure the associated PivotTable and review the resulting changes in the PivotChart.
2. Sort or filter the data directly in the PivotTable report and review the resulting changes in the PivotChart.
3. Sort or filter the data from the **PivotChart Filter Pane.**
   a. Select the PivotChart.
   b. If the **PivotChart Filter Pane** does not appear, on the **PivotChart Tools Analyze** contextual tab, in the **Show/Hide** group, click **PivotChart Filter.** (You can show or hide the **PivotTable Field List** pane from this tab as well.)
   c. In the **PivotChart Filter Pane**, use the **Report Filter, Axis Fields (Categories)**, and **Legend Fields (Series)** drop-down lists to sort and filter the data, and then review the resulting changes in the PivotChart.
4. To analyze new data, rebuild the PivotTable and associated PivotChart.
   a. On the **PivotChart Tools Analyze** contextual tab, in the **Data** group, click the **Clear** drop-down and select **Clear All.**
   b. Use the **PivotTable Field List** pane to reconstruct the PivotTable.
   c. Review the results in the PivotChart. If the changes do not immediately appear in the PivotChart, on the **PivotChart Tools Analyze** contextual tab, click **Refresh.**

Procedure Reference: Format a PivotChart

To format a PivotChart:

1. In the worksheet, select the PivotChart.
2. On the **Ribbon**, select the desired **PivotChart Tools** contextual tab: **Design, Layout**, or **Format.**

3. On the selected contextual tab, in the desired group, select the appropriate command to format the PivotChart.

Creating PivotTables from an Existing PivotTable

A PivotChart can be created from an existing PivotTable by choosing the **PivotChart** option in the **Tools** group on the **PivotTable Tools Options** contextual tab.

ACTIVITY 4-3
Creating a PivotChart

Before You Begin:

My Shipping.xlsx is open.

Scenario:

The sales manager at Everything For Coffee LLC has asked you to create a column chart based on the data that is in the Invoices sheet to show the sales people how they have been doing with their sales for different food products in different countries. Instead of creating multiple column charts, you decide to present the data in a simple format using a PivotChart that can filter the details of sales by country and product.

---

1. Create a PivotChart.

    a. Select the **Invoices** worksheet tab.

    b. On the **Insert** tab, in the **Tables** group, click the **PivotTable** drop-down and select **PivotChart**.

    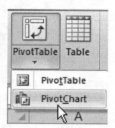

    c. In the **Create PivotTable with PivotChart** dialog box, verify that the **Select a table or range** and **New Worksheet** options are selected and click **OK**.

    d. In the **PivotTable Field List** pane, in the **Choose fields to add to report** list box, drag the **Salesperson** field to the **Axis Fields (Categories)** box.

    e. In the **Choose fields to add to report** list box, drag the **Quantity** field to the **Values** box.

    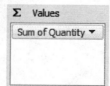

f. Notice that a PivotTable has been created in the worksheet along with the PivotChart. Verify that the vertical axis displays a range of amounts from 0 through 12000.

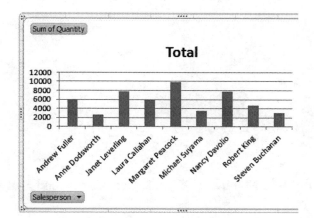

g. Select the border of the PivotChart and place it below the PivotTable for better view.

2. Change the chart title to Salesperson's Performance.

a. In the PivotChart, click the **Chart Title** to select it.

b. Select the text and enter ***Salesperson's Performance***

c. Click the chart area to deselect the chart title.

3. Create a PivotChart report filter to filter the report by country and then by product, to display the total quantity for products sold by each salesperson in a country.

a. Drag the **Country** field to the **Report Filter** box.

b. Drag the **Product Name** field to the **Report Filter** box below the **Country** field.

c. On the PivotChart, in the **Country** drop-down list, select **Germany** and click **OK**.

d. Verify that the vertical axis now displays amounts that range from 0 through 2500 to reflect the range of amounts sold to **Germany** by different salespersons.

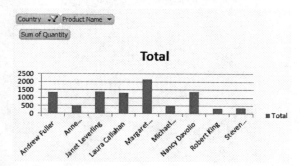

e. On the PivotChart, in the **Product Name** drop-down list, select **Aniseed Syrup** and click **OK.**

f. Verify that both the PivotTable and the PivotChart now display the **Sum of Quantity** for the product **Aniseed Syrup** in **Germany** for different salespersons.

g. On the PivotChart, in the **Country** drop-down list, select **Brazil**, and click **OK.**

h. Observe that there is no sales data available for the product **Aniseed Syrup** in **Brazil.**

i. On the PivotChart, in the **Product Name** drop-down list, select **Chang** and click **OK.**

j. Verify that the vertical axis now displays the **Sum of Quantity** for the product **Chang** in **Brazil** for different salespersons.

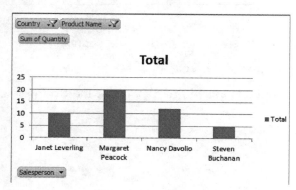

k. Close the **PivotTable Field List** pane.

4. Format the PivotChart.

a. If necessary, click the border of the PivotChart to select the chart.

b. On the **PivotChart Tools Design** contextual tab, in the **Type** group, click **Change Chart Type.**

c. In the **Change Chart Type** dialog box, in the right pane, in the **Column** section, in the first row, select **3–D Clustered Column**, which is the fourth chart type from left, and click **OK.**

d.   Observe that the 2–D chart is converted to **3–D Clustered Column** chart.

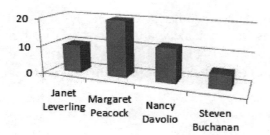

e.   In the **Chart Styles** group, click the **More** button.

f.   In the displayed gallery, select a style of your choice.

g.   Save and close the file.

Lesson 4 Follow-up

In this lesson, you used PivotTables and PivotCharts to perform data analysis. You also applied Slicers to the PivotTable to filter data. These tools enable you to interactively analyze and manipulate large amounts of data in sophisticated ways.

1. **How will your use of PivotTables and PivotCharts improve the way you analyze and display data?**

2. **What do you think are the advantages of using Slicers with PivotTables?**

5 | Inserting Graphic Objects

Lesson Time: 1 hour(s)

Lesson Objectives:

In this lesson, you will insert and modify graphic objects in a worksheet.

You will:

- Insert and modify pictures and clip art graphics.
- Draw and modify shapes.
- Illustrate workflow using SmartArt graphics.
- Layer and group graphic objects.

Introduction

You created and formatted charts for presenting data graphically. In addition to charts based on worksheet data, Microsoft Office Excel enables you to create a number of other types of independent graphic objects to illustrate data. In this lesson, you will insert graphic objects to further enhance the presentation of data.

A spreadsheet that contains only tables and numeric data will look monotonous and uninteresting. When you use graphic elements in a spreadsheet, you will be able to draw users' attention to specific areas of the spreadsheet. You can also enhance the look and visual appeal of your data with corporate logos, diagrams, and other graphic elements.

TOPIC A

Insert and Modify Pictures and ClipArt

In this lesson, you will insert various graphic objects into worksheets. The most common types of graphical objects are screenshots, pictures, and ClipArt graphics. In this topic, you will insert graphics into your worksheets and modify them.

To make your worksheets attractive, you may want to add graphic objects to them. The screenshot capturing feature in Microsoft Office 2010 allows you to capture the screen of the active desktop or other applications and embed it into worksheets. However, if you have a selection of graphics that already exists, such as ClipArt, you can quickly choose and insert them wherever required.

Graphic Objects

Definition:

A *graphic object* is a visual element that can be inserted into a worksheet. Graphics can be inserted anywhere in a worksheet and are not associated with a specific cell. When a graphic object is selected, small sizing handles indicate the object's borders. All graphic objects have rotation handles, and some even have adjustment handles. Graphics can be moved, copied, or resized. Some graphics, including *pictures* and *clip art,* are premade and inserted from existing files. Other graphics, such as *SmartArt,* and *shapes,* are created from scratch.

Example:

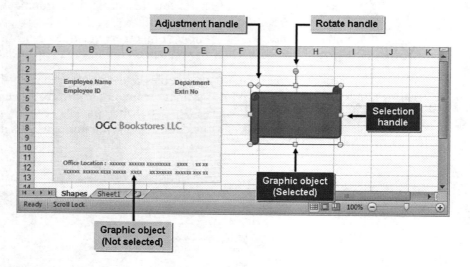

Figure 5-1: *Graphic objects on a worksheet.*

Pictures and Clip Art

Inserting pictures and clip art graphics in a worksheet may help in making effective presentations.

Object Type	Description
Picture	An image that is stored in any one of a number of graphics file formats. Pictures tend to be complex, photorealistic, two- or three-dimensional images. You can enhance pictures by changing their styles and effects such as shadow and glow. In addition, you can add borders and adjust their size, or apply artistic effects to modify the appearance of pictures.
ClipArt	Simple, stylized, built-in two-dimensional drawings that can be inserted in your worksheet. In addition to standard images, ClipArt also includes photographs, movies, and sounds. Like pictures, ClipArt graphics too can be resized and modified. A collection of ClipArt objects is available in the **Microsoft Clip Organizer** application that ships with the Office 2010 package and the collection can be enhanced by downloading more ClipArt objects from the web or other available sources. Microsoft provides a collection of both free and paid ClipArt objects on the Microsoft Office Online or Office.com website, which can be accessed at **http://office.microsoft.com/en-us/images/default.aspx**.

The Screen Capping Tool

Like all other Microsoft Office 2010 applications, Excel allows users to capture screenshots of the desktop, open windows, or portions of open windows using the **Screenshot** button. Once inserted into a worksheet, a screenshot can be treated like any other picture graphic. Screenshots are useful for capturing information that might change or expire after some time; for example, stock prices or currency conversion rates. Screenshots are also useful for capturing the information displayed on certain web pages and other applications that cannot be saved in a compatible format on the computer.

The Remove Background Tab

You can remove unwanted portions of screenshots using the **Remove Background** tab in the **Adjust** group on the **Picture Tools Format** contextual tab. By using this tab, you can retain only those portions of a screenshot that are required.

Picture Formatting Options

You can add various visual effects to graphical elements such as screenshots, pictures, and ClipArt. You can recolor a graphic to give it a grayscale or sepia tone effect; increase or decrease the brightness or contrast of an image; choose and apply image styles from the **Quick Styles** gallery; or add 3-D, shadow, and reflection effects. In addition, you can modify the transparency of images, add artistic effects or borders, and adjust the size of the image. Most of the graphic formatting options are available on the **Picture Tools Format** contextual tab.

The Artistic Effects Feature

Excel 2010 allows you to modify pictures by applying artistic effects to them. Artistic effects can be applied to make a photo look more like a sketch, drawing, or painting. Because only one artistic effect can be applied at a time, applying a different effect will remove the previously applied effect. The **Artistic Effects** drop-down is located in the **Adjust** group on the **Picture Tools Format** contextual tab.

How to Insert and Modify Pictures and Clip Art Graphics

Procedure Reference: Insert Clip Art in a Worksheet

To insert clip art in a worksheet:

1. On the **Insert** tab, in the **Illustrations** group, click **ClipArt.**

2. In the **ClipArt** task pane, in the **Search For** text box, type a word or phrase that describes the required ClipArt graphic.

3. If necessary, in the **Search In** drop-down list, check the check boxes for the appropriate collections.

4. If necessary, check Include Office.com Content to include the ClipArt objects from the site **http://office.microsoft.com/en-us/images/default.aspx** in the search.

5. If necessary, in the **Results Should Be** drop-down list, check the check boxes for the appropriate media type(s) and click **Go.**

 By default, all media types are checked.

6. Select the location in the worksheet where you want to insert the ClipArt object.

7. Click the ClipArt object you want to insert.

Procedure Reference: Insert a Picture from a File

To insert a picture from a file:

1. Select the location on the worksheet where you want to insert the picture.

2. On the **Insert** tab, in the **Illustrations** group, click **Picture.**

3. Insert the picture.

- In the **Insert Picture** dialog box, navigate to the desired folder location, select the required picture, and click **Insert.**

- Or, double-click the required picture.

Procedure Reference: Modify a Graphic

To modify a graphic:

1. If necessary, select the graphic.

2. Modify the graphic.

- To apply a style, on the **Picture Tools Format** contextual tab, in the **Picture Styles** group, select a style or click the **More** button to display additional styles.

- To resize a graphic, drag the graphic's sizing handles, or use the options in the **Size** group on the **Picture Tools Format** contextual tab to specify the height and width values.

- To change a graphic's shape, on the **Picture Tools Format** contextual tab, in the **Picture Styles** group, click **Picture Shape** and select a shape.

- To apply a border, on the **Picture Tools Format** contextual tab, in the **Picture Styles** group, click **Picture Border** and select a new border property.

- To apply a picture effect, on the **Picture Tools Format** contextual tab, in the **Picture Style** group, click **Picture Effects** and select the desired effect.

- To adjust overall picture appearance, on the **Picture Tools Format** contextual tab, make **Brightness**, **Contrast**, and **Recolor** selections from the galleries in the **Adjust** group.

Aspect Ratio

The ratio of height to width of an image is known as its aspect ratio. While modifying the **Shape Height**, Excel automatically updates the **Shape Width** field to maintain the original aspect ratio. The user can change the **Shape Width** value if required.

Procedure Reference: Add Artistic Effects to Images

To add artistic effects to the images:

1. Select the graphic.
2. On the **Picture Tools Format** contextual tab, in the **Adjust** group, click the **Artistic Effects** drop-down.
3. From the gallery, select an artistic effect.
4. If necessary, select the image, and from the artistic effects gallery, select another artistic effect to apply it to the image.

Procedure Reference: Insert a Screenshot

To insert a screenshot in a worksheet:

1. Open the application window whose screenshot you want to capture.
2. Open the worksheet in which you want to add the screenshot.
3. Select the location on the worksheet where you want to insert the screenshot.
4. On the **Insert** tab, in the **Illustrations** group, click the **Screenshot** drop-down arrow.
5. Insert the screenshot.

- To capture and add the entire application window, from the **Available Windows** gallery, select the thumbnail of the application window.

- To capture and add part of the window, click **Screen Clipping,** and when the pointer gets displayed as a cross, press and hold the left mouse button and drag to select the area of your screen that you want to capture.

Procedure Reference: Insert a Desktop Screenshot

To insert a screenshot of the desktop:

1. Minimize all open windows.

2. Select the location on the worksheet where you want to insert the screenshot.

3. On the **Insert** tab, in the **Illustrations** group, click the **Screenshot** drop-down arrow and choose **Screen Clipping.**

4. When the pointer gets displayed as a cross, click and drag to select the area of desktop that you want to capture.

Procedure Reference: Add a Background to a Worksheet

To add a background to a worksheet:

1. Select the worksheet for which you want to apply the background.

2. On the **Page Layout** tab, in the **Page Setup** group, click **Background.**

3. Select the graphic to be inserted as the background and click **Insert.**

Removing a Background

The background of an image can be removed by using the **Delete Background** button on the **Page Setup** group of the **Page Layout** tab. The **Delete Background** button will appear only when there is a background applied to the worksheet.

ACTIVITY 5-1
Inserting and Modifying a Picture in a Worksheet

Data Files:

New Employees List.xlsx

Scenario:

As the human resources manager at OGC Stores, you are about to forward a list of new employees to the administration department for printing their business cards. You want the business cards to be printed in the new format. So you decided to include a graphic of the business card at the bottom of the list.

1. Insert the visiting card graphic onto the Employees' worksheet.

   a. From the C:\084577Data\Inserting Graphic Objects folder, open the New Employees List.xlsx file.

   b. In the **Employees** worksheet, scroll down and select cell **B26**.

   c. On the **Insert** tab, in the **Illustrations** group, click **Picture.**

   d. In the **Insert Picture** dialog box, navigate to the C:\084577Data\Inserting Graphic Objects folder.

   e. Double-click the **Visiting Card.jpg** graphic to insert it into the worksheet.

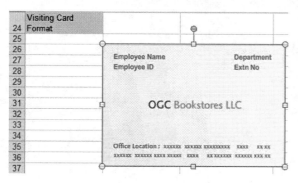

2. Resize the picture so that it is 3 inches in height and 4.5 inches in width.

   a. With the graphic selected, on the **Picture Tools Format** contextual tab, in the **Size** group, in the **Shape Height** spin box, select the existing value and enter *3*

    b.   Verify that the value in the **Shape Width** spin box automatically changes to **4.5** to maintain the aspect ratio of the original.

3.   Apply a picture border.

    a.   In the **Picture Styles** group, click the **Picture Border** drop-down.

    b.   In the **Theme Colors** section of the gallery, in the first row, fourth column, select the **Dark Blue, Text 2** color.

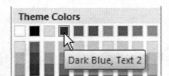

    c.   In the **Picture Styles** group, click the **Picture Border** drop-down.

    d.   Choose **Weight→1 1/2 pt** to apply the new border.

    e.   Click anywhere on the worksheet to deselect the graphic.

    f.   Observe that the effects have been applied to the graphic. Save the file as *My New Employees List* and close it.

TOPIC B

Draw and Modify Shapes

In the previous topic, you enhanced your worksheet by adding graphic objects to it. You can also create custom graphics easily by using Excel's library of lines and shapes. In this topic, you will draw lines and shapes on a worksheet.

Lines and shapes help to add emphasis or draw attention to a particular area of a worksheet. Instead of trying to create complex graphic elements, you can often achieve the effects you want by working with the lines and shapes available in Excel.

Shapes

Definition:

Shapes are simple geometric objects that you can draw and modify as needed to enhance your worksheets. You can add a single shape to your worksheet or combine multiple shapes to create your own complex shapes. After you add a shape, you can enhance it by adding text, bullets, numbering, and Quick Styles.

Example:

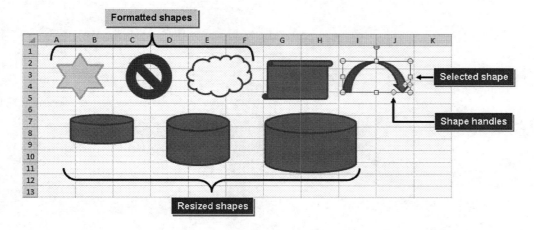

Figure 5-2: Shapes emphasize certain areas of a worksheet.

Types of Shapes

There are many ready-made shapes that you can quickly insert into your worksheet. These include lines, arrows and connectors, rectangles and other geometric shapes, block-style arrows, mathematical symbols for equations, flowchart elements, stars and banners, and callouts in various forms.

How to Draw and Modify Shapes

Procedure Reference: Insert and Modify a Shape

To insert and modify a shape:

1. On the **Ribbon**, select the **Insert** tab.

2. In the **Illustrations** group, click **Shapes** to display a list of shapes.

3. In the **Shapes** gallery, select a shape.

4. Position the mouse pointer in the worksheet.

5. Draw the shape.

    *   Click to drop a pre-sized shape onto the worksheet.

    *   Or, click and drag to draw the shape.

6. If necessary, modify the appearance of the shape.

    *   Drag the resizing handles to change the size of the shape.

    *   Use the **Rotation** handle to turn the shape.

    *   Right-click and choose **Format Shape** to display the **Format Shape** dialog box to configure various shape settings.

7. If necessary, on the **Page Layout** tab, in the **Sheet Options** group, in the **Gridlines** section, uncheck **View** to remove the gridlines.

ACTIVITY 5-2
Drawing and Modifying Shapes

Data Files:

Sales Analysis

Scenario:

Being the regional manager for OGC Bookstores (European region), you are going to present the sales trend for the last fiscal in the annual board meeting. The company managed to obtain high profits in the last fiscal in the region, and you have been asked to share how it was made possible. You decide to present the process flow using a diagram for better visual appeal, and because you already have a sales report for the last fiscal in a worksheet, you include the diagram in the same workbook on a different worksheet to avoid switching between different applications during the presentation.

1. Insert the necessary shapes in the worksheet.

   a. From the C:\084577Data\Inserting Graphic Objects folder, open the Sales Analysis.xlsx file.

   b. Select **Sheet2.**

   c. On the **Insert** tab, in the **Illustrations** group, click the **Shapes** drop down.

   d. In the **Shapes** gallery, in the **Flowchart** section, select **Flowchart:Data**, which is the fourth option in the first row.

   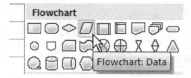

   e. On the worksheet, click cell **C5** to place the shape on the worksheet.

   f. Resize the graphic such that the right end extends up to the end of column F.

g. Press **Ctrl+D** to create another similar shape and position it at the beginning of column **K**.

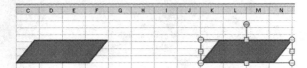

 Resize objects using the sizing handles to ensure that the shapes are proportional.

h. Similarly, create two rectangle shapes and resize them so that they cover the ranges **B14:F17** and **J14:N17** respectively.

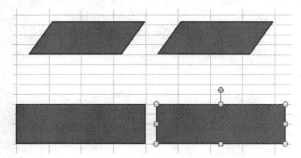

i. Insert a **Flowchart: Terminator** shape that covers the range **G20:I23**.

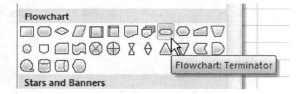

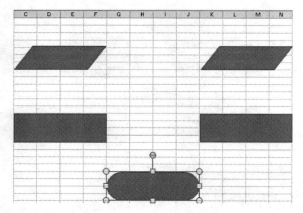

2. Add text to the shapes.

a. On the **Insert** tab, in the **Text** group, click **Text Box** and select the leftmost rhombus to insert a text box on the shape.

b. On the **Home** tab, in the **Font** group, from the **Font Size** drop-down list, select **16.**

c. In the **Alignment** group, from the top row, click **Middle Align**, and from the bottom row, click **Center.**

d. In the text box, type *Increase in Sales by 30%*

e. Select the rightmost rhombus, set the font size to 16 with middle and center alignment, and enter the text *Reduction in Overheads by 40%*

f. In the left and right rectangles, set the font size to 16 with middle and center alignment, and enter *Increased Market Share* and *Increased Productivity* respectively.

g. In the oval shape, set the font size to 16 with middle and center alignment, and enter *Increase in Profit*

3. Add Arrow shapes to link the shape boxes.

a. On the **Insert** tab, in the **Illustrations** group, click **Shapes**, and then in the **Block Arrows** section, in the first row, select the fourth arrow shape to select the **Down Arrow** shape.

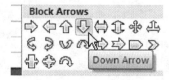

b.   Click cell **D9** to place the **Down Arrow** shape on the spreadsheet.

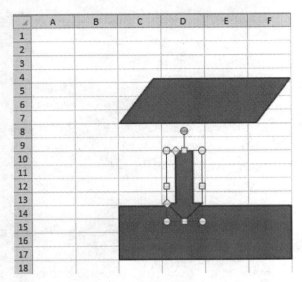

c.   If necessary, select the **Down Arrow** shape to display its positioning handles.

d.   Size the shape so that its outer rectangular border traces all cells in the range **D9:E13** partially.

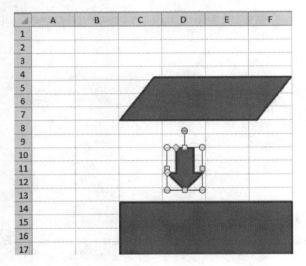

e. Similarly, add a down arrow shape for linking the shape boxes on the right side.

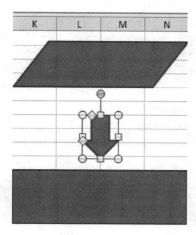

f. On the **Insert** tab, in the **Illustrations** group, click **Shapes**, and then in the **Block Arrows** section, select the **Bent-Up Arrow** shape, which is the last shape in the first row.

g. Select cell **E19.** The **Ctrl** key is pressed, press **D** to create another shape.

h. Rotate the shapes to the correct orientation using their rotation handles and rectangular borders and place them such that each one links a rectangle shape with the oval shape.

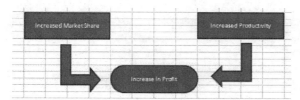

i. On the **Page Layout** tab, in the **Sheet Options** group, in the **Gridlines** section, uncheck **View** to remove the gridlines.

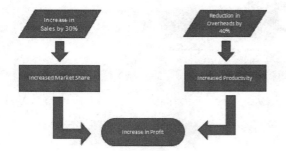

j. Save the file as ***My Sales Analysis*** and close it.

TOPIC C

Illustrate Workflow Using SmartArt Graphics

In the previous topics, you inserted default graphics and drew simple shapes. If these types of graphics do not meet your needs, you can insert a more complex category of graphic object called SmartArt. In this topic, you will use SmartArt graphics to illustrate the workflow of a process.

You might need to present a complicated workflow process or illustrate a network diagram. Even if you do not have much time or particular graphic design skills, you can use SmartArt graphics to quickly create a comprehensive workflow diagram or any other graphical representation that involves relationships, sequence, or hierarchy.

SmartArt Graphics

Definition:

A *SmartArt graphic* is a custom-made visual representation of the relationships between data, events, or ideas. A SmartArt graphic combines graphic objects with text and connector symbols to create complex custom illustrations. Once you insert a SmartArt graphic, you can change its structure and layout, add and customize text, and modify the format and appearance of each element and of the SmartArt object as a whole.

Example:

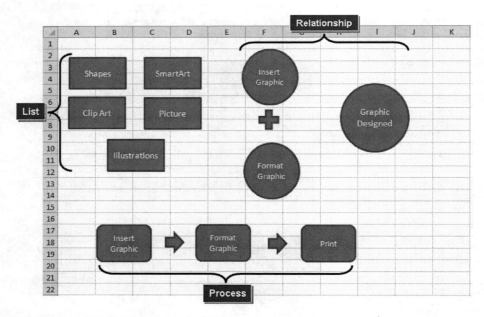

Figure 5-3: *SmartArt graphics provide a visual representation of the relationships between data, events, or ideas.*

The Choose a SmartArt Graphic Dialog Box

The **Choose a SmartArt Graphic** dialog box, in the **Illustrations** group on the **Insert** tab, displays SmartArt layouts in eight categories: List, Process, Cycle, Hierarchy, Relationship, Matrix, Pyramid, and Picture. Each category contains a variety of layouts for showing the appropriate type of relationship, sequence, or hierarchy between the components of a SmartArt graphic.

How to Illustrate Workflow Using SmartArt Graphics

Procedure Reference: Insert a SmartArt Graphic

To insert a SmartArt graphic:

1. On the **Ribbon**, on the **Insert** tab, in the **Illustrations** group, click **SmartArt.**

2. In the **Choose A SmartArt Graphic** dialog box, in the left pane, select a graphic category.

3. In the center pane, select the **SmartArt** graphic thumbnail. The right pane in the **SmartArt Graphic** dialog box provides descriptive information on the currently selected graphic thumbnail.

4. Click **OK.**

Procedure Reference: Add Text to SmartArt Objects

To add text to SmartArt objects:

1. Select the SmartArt object. For some object types, a text pane with **[Text]** placeholders will appear on the left of the object. If the text pane does not appear, click the **Text Pane** control button located on the left border of the SmartArt graphic.

2. Enter the SmartArt text.

    ●   Click the **[Text]** placeholder in the text pane and type the desired text.

    ●   Or, click the **[Text]** placeholder in the process step box and type the desired text.

Procedure Reference: Add or Reposition SmartArt Shapes

To add or reposition SmartArt shapes:

1. Select the SmartArt graphic.

2. Select one of the existing shapes.

3. On the **SmartArt Tools Design** contextual tab, in the **Create Graphic** group, click the **Add Shape** drop-down and then choose **Add Shape After, Add Shape Before, Add Shape Above**, or **Add Shape Below.**

4. To reposition a shape, drag it to the desired position.

5. If necessary, in the text pane, click at the end of a text item corresponding to a process step and press **Enter** to add a new step in the process.

Procedure Reference: Format SmartArt Graphics

To format SmartArt graphics:

1. If necessary, select the SmartArt graphic.

2. To apply a SmartArt style, on the **SmartArt Tools Design** contextual tab, select a style from the **SmartArt Styles** group.

3. To change the overall layout, on the **SmartArt Tools Design** contextual tab, select a layout from the **Layouts** group.

4. To format individual objects, select the objects, and make the appropriate selections on the **SmartArt Tools Format** contextual tab. You can change the shape or size, apply a style, and change the shape fill, outline, or effects.

ACTIVITY 5-3
Inserting a SmartArt Graphic

Data Files:

Inventory.xlsx

Scenario:

As the incharge for managing the inventory of OGC Constructions, you have presented the inventory status report to the board. You are also going to share the inventory management process with the new employees and show a sample inventory report to them. You decide to spruce up the Excel workbook containing the inventory report by inserting a SmartArt graphic.

1. On the Inventory Management Process worksheet, insert a SmartArt graphic representing the inventory management process.

   a. From the C:\084577Data\Inserting Graphic Objects folder, open the Inventory.xlsx file.

   b. If necessary, select the **Inventory Management Process** tab.

   c. On the **Insert** tab, in the **Illustrations** group, click **SmartArt.**

   d. In the **Choose a SmartArt Graphic** dialog box, in the left pane, select **Process.**

   e. In the center pane, in the first column, select **Continuous Block Process**, the first option in third row.

   f. Verify that an explanation of the SmartArt graphic is displayed in the right pane and click **OK.**

2. Enter the text for the process steps.

   a. In the **Type your text here** pane, in the first bullet point, type *Budgetary Planning*

   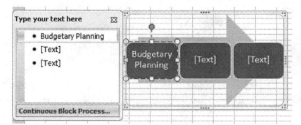

b. Observe that the text automatically gets added to the first text box of the SmartArt graphic.

c. In the second bullet point, type **Needs Identification**

d. In the third bullet point, type ***Finalization of Agreements with Vendors***

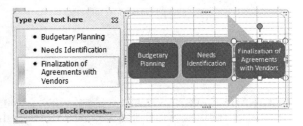

3. Add new steps after the third step.

a. In the **Type your text here** pane, if necessary, place the cursor at the end of the text in the third bullet point and press **Enter** to define a new text box.

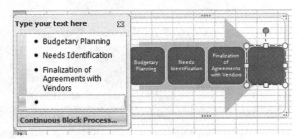

b. In the fourth bullet point, type ***Order Placement***

c. Add two new process steps after the fourth step and enter the text ***Goods Receipt and Invoicing*** and ***Storage and Maintenance***

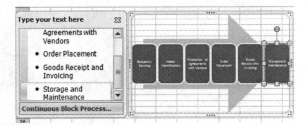

d. Close the **Type your text here** pane.

4. Modify the SmartArt graphic's size and remove the gridlines.

a. Place the mouse pointer at the top-left corner of the SmartArt graphic's border and resize the graphic such that the border extends up to cell **B3.**

b. Place the mouse pointer on the right border of the SmartArt graphic and resize the graphic such that the right border extends up to the right end of column **N.**

c. On the **Page Layout** tab, in the **Sheet Options** group, in the **Gridlines** section, uncheck **View** to remove the gridlines.

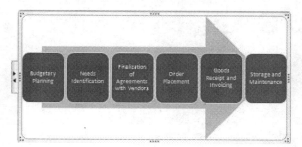

5. Change the colors of the process steps.

a. On the **SmartArt Tools Design** contextual tab, in the **SmartArt Styles** group, click the **Change Colors** drop-down.

b. In the **Colorful** section, select the fourth color scheme to apply the **Colorful Range – Accent Colors 4 to 5** color scheme to the SmartArt graphic.

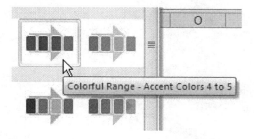

6. Apply the 3-D Inset SmartArt style to the SmartArt graphic.

a. In the **SmartArt Styles** group, click the **More** button.

b. In the **3-D** section, in the second row, select the second SmartArt style to select the **Brick Scene** style.

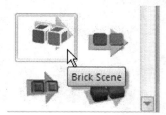

c. Save the file as *My Inventory Management Process* and close it.

TOPIC D

Layer and Group Graphic Objects

You inserted many types of graphic objects. If you have several graphic objects on a worksheet, you might want to adjust how they are displayed in relation to one another, or manage them as a unit. In this topic, you will layer and group graphic objects.

Your worksheet may require you to create more complex designs, integrating separate graphics within a narrow space. To control the position of those graphics, you will need to use layers, as well as form groups of graphics when you want to move multiple layered images simultaneously on the page.

Layering

Definition:

Layering is a method of displaying graphics that overlap other graphics in a specific order. Each graphic object is a separate layer. The layer order and opacity determines which part of a graphic object is visible.

Example:

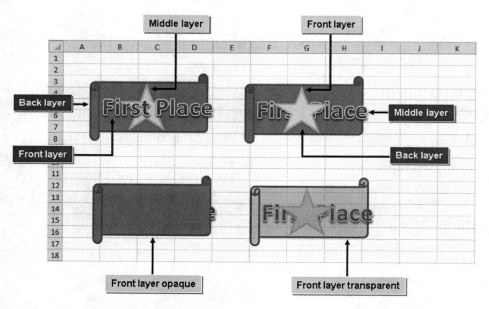

Figure 5-4: *Layering allows you to arrange multiple objects.*

Grouping

Definition:

Grouping is a method of connecting multiple graphics so that you can manipulate them as a unit. A grouped object has its own selection handles that can be used to copy, move, and resize the combined graphic as a single item. You can ungroup a graphic if you need to format or modify individual graphic objects separately. A grouped graphic object can contain other grouped graphics.

Example:

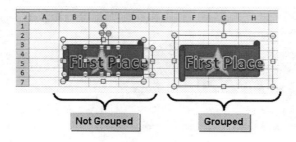

Figure 5-5: Multiple objects can be grouped into a single object.

How to Layer and Group Graphic Objects

Procedure Reference: Change the Layering Order

To change the layering order:

1. Select the object you would like to change in the layering order.

2. To bring the object forward, on the **Drawing Tools Format** contextual tab, in the **Arrange** group, click the **Bring To Front** drop-down list and select the appropriate action.

    ● Choose **Bring To Front** to bring the object to the top layer.

    ● Or, choose **Bring Forward** to bring the object forward one layer.

     To bring the object to the top layer or send the object to the bottom layer, you can click **Bring To Front** or **Send To Back** in the **Arrange** group.

3. To send the object backward, on the **Drawing Tools Format** contextual tab, in the **Arrange** group, click the **Send To Back** drop-down list arrow and select the appropriate action.

    ● Choose **Send To Back** to send the object to the bottom layer.

    ● Or, choose **Send Backward** to send the object backward one layer.

Procedure Reference: Group or Ungroup Graphic Objects

To group or ungroup graphic objects:

1. Hold down **Ctrl** and then select the graphic objects you want to group.

2. Verify that the positioning handles appear for each object you select.

3. On the **Drawing Tools Format** contextual tab, in the **Arrange** group, click the **Group** drop-down and select **Group.**

4. To ungroup grouped graphics, select the group, and on the **Drawing Tools Format** contextual tab, in the **Arrange** group, click the **Group** drop-down and select **Ungroup.**

Duplicating and Copying Objects

If you need to make copies of graphic objects, you can copy and paste them. However, Excel also offers you the ability to create duplicates of graphic objects in a single step. To duplicate an object quickly, select the object and press **Ctrl+D.** A duplicate of the original image will appear over the original; you can drag the duplicate to position it to meet your needs.

ACTIVITY 5-4
Grouping Graphics

Scenario:

OGC Bookstores wants to create a new hologram that will be attached to all books and DVDs. Your company has asked the employees to submit their suggestions. Because you frequently use Excel for creating reports and don't have any image editing software in your system, you decide to create a draft design in Excel and pass it on to the media development team. You have been trying to develop a simple layered graphic that consists of a stack of books behind a globe image. To create the stack of books, you decide to use the duplication feature to duplicate a book graphic.

---

1. Insert a book graphic in to the worksheet and duplicate it.

   a. Open an Excel workbook.

   b. Select cell **C3**.

   c. On the **Insert** tab, in the **Illustrations** group, click **Picture.**

   d. In the **Insert Picture** dialog box, navigate to the C:\084577Data\Inserting Graphic Objects folder.

   e. Double-click the **Book.jpg** graphic to insert it into the worksheet.

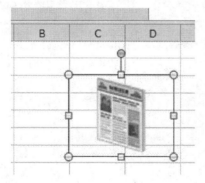

   f. Press **Ctrl+D** to create a duplicate image of the book.

g. Observe that the duplicate image overlaps the original graphic.

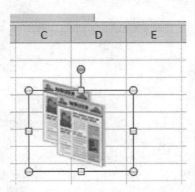

2. Insert a globe graphic into the worksheet.

   a. Select cell **F3.**

   b. On the **Insert** tab, in the **Illustrations** group, click **Picture.**

   c. In the **Insert Picture** dialog box, navigate to the C:\084577Data\Inserting Graphic Objects folder.

   d. Double-click the **Globe.jpg** graphic to insert it into the worksheet.

   e. Drag the Globe graphic and position it above the stacked books.

3. Group the shapes.

   a. Select the Book graphic at the end, hold down **Ctrl**, and then select the second Book graphic and the Globe graphic.

   b. Observe that separate positioning handles appear for each selected shape. On the **Page Layout** tab, in the **Arrange** group, click the **Group** drop-down and select **Group.**

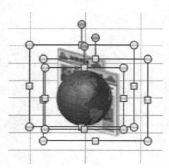

c. Verify that a single positioning handle appears for the grouped object.

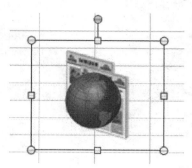

d. On the **Page Layout** tab, in the **Sheet Options** group, in the **Gridlines** section, uncheck **View** to remove the gridlines.

e. Save the file as *My Logo* and close it.

Lesson 5 Follow-up

In this lesson, you added graphic elements to a worksheet. Graphic elements will make a worksheet look more professional and draw attention to certain areas of the worksheet that would otherwise be hard to identify.

1. **What sort of graphic element would you include on the first worksheet of your company's annual sales report?**

2. **In what situations would you need to capture screenshots of applications?**

6 | Customizing and Enhancing the Excel Environment

Lesson Time: 45 minutes

Lesson Objectives:

In this lesson, you will customize and enhance workbooks and the Microsoft Office Excel environment.

You will:

- Customize the Excel environment.
- Customize workbooks.
- Manage themes.
- Create and use templates.

Introduction

You inserted a number of components in a workbook to increase the complexity and sophistication of content within it. You can extend the level of customization to apply to the Excel environment, so that all your workbooks have rich features and sophistication. In this lesson, you will enhance the appearance and functionality of the Excel environment.

The customization options in Excel enable you to organize the work environment to suit specific needs and preferences. You can include comments, hyperlinks, watermarks, and background pictures to your worksheet and make it more functional. You can also save your functional worksheet as a template for all other worksheets.

TOPIC A

Customize the Excel Environment

In this lesson, you will customize and enhance workbooks and the Excel environment. You also need to ensure that the application works at its optimum best even after you have made enhancements to it. In this topic, you will customize the Excel interface to suit your preferences.

Excel provides you with many helpful features that are available by default on the Excel interface. In some cases, you may need to work with other Excel features that may not be very noticeable. In order to make these features readily available, Excel provides options that enable you to display the elements you require and hide the ones you do not frequently use. This gives you the advantage of optimizing the functionality of your workbook. You can choose and implement only those functions that you may want to work with while disabling the rest.

General Options in Excel

The **General** category in the **Excel Options** dialog box enables you to personalize a number of common environment settings, including the display settings of features and interface elements, and the default settings of new workbooks.

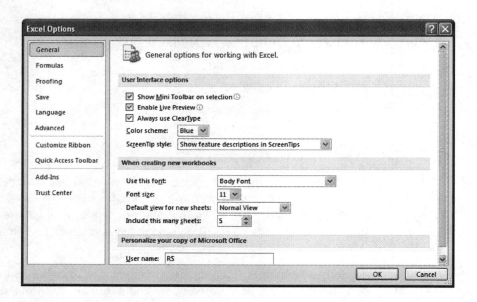

Figure 6-1: *The various customization options in the General category.*

Items on the General Category

The **General** category in the **Excel Options** dialog box includes different customization options.

Option	Description
Show Mini Toolbar on selection	When checked, Excel will show the Mini Toolbar when you select text, thereby providing quick access to the formatting tools.

Option	Description
Enable Live Preview	When checked, Excel will show a preview of how a feature can affect the document as you move the pointer over the different choices.
Always use ClearType	When checked, enables the ClearType font technology. ClearType improves the appearance of on-screen text on Liquid Crystal Display (LCD) monitors, such as some laptop screens.
Color scheme	This drop-down list enables you to select a color scheme for the Microsoft Office environment.
ScreenTip style	This drop-down list enables you to choose the display type for the ScreenTip. You can show or hide feature descriptions in ScreenTips, or you can turn off ScreenTips entirely.
Use this font	This drop-down list enables you to select a font to use when you create a new workbook.
Font size	This drop-down list enables you to select a font size to use when you create a new workbook.
Default view for new sheets	This drop-down list enables you to set the default display of a new worksheet to **Normal View**, **Page Break Preview**, or **Page Layout View**. The default is **Normal View.**
Include this many sheets	This spin box enables you to specify the number of sheets to include every time you create a new workbook. The default is three sheets.
User name	Enables you to personalize your copy of Excel by entering your user name.

Color Schemes

Definition:

A *color scheme* is a defined set of colors used for controlling the overall appearance of the Excel application. Although the default color scheme is blue, you can select from other color schemes. The appearance of components such as tabs, toolbars, and buttons will depend upon the color scheme selected.

Example:

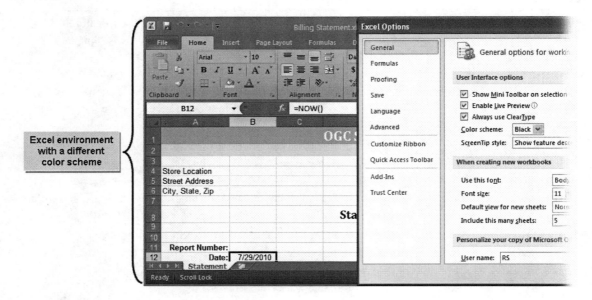

Figure 6-2: The color scheme determines the appearance of the interface.

How to Customize the Excel Environment

Procedure Reference: Customize General Options

To customize general options:

1. On the **File** tab, select **Options.**
2. In the **Excel Options** dialog box, in the left pane, select the **General** category.
3. In the **General options for working with Excel** section, check or uncheck the desired options.

    ●   Select a color scheme from the **Color scheme** drop-down list.

    ●   Select a ScreenTip style from the **ScreenTip style** drop-down list.

    ●   In the **When creating new workbooks** section, use the drop-down lists to select the default font, font size, view, and number of sheets for new workbooks.

    ●   In the **Personalize your copy of Microsoft Office** section, type your user name.

4. Click **OK** in the **Excel Options** dialog box to apply the changes.

Procedure Reference: Minimize or Restore the Ribbon

To minimize or restore the Ribbon:

 You can minimize the Ribbon to reveal more of the worksheet work area. When the Ribbon is minimized, the commands are hidden and only the tabs show.

1. If desired, minimize the Ribbon.

    - Double-click the active Ribbon tab.

    - Or, on the **Quick Access Toolbar**, click the **Minimize the Ribbon** drop-down arrow near the **Help** button.

    - Or, press **Ctrl+F1.**

    - Or, right-click the Ribbon and choose **Minimize the Ribbon.**

2. To display commands on the Ribbon while it is minimized, click any tab. The Ribbon will minimize again as soon as you press **Esc** or click away from the Ribbon.

3. If desired, restore the Ribbon.

    - Double-click any Ribbon tab.

    - Or, on the **Quick Access** toolbar, click the **Expand the Ribbon** button near the **Help** button.

    - Or, press **Ctrl+F1.**

ACTIVITY 6-1
Customizing Display Options

Before You Begin:

Open an Excel worksheet.

Scenario:

Your organization has recently upgraded to Excel 2010. You want to explore its interface and make some changes to the user interface so that it is visually appealing and suits your personal preferences.

1. Modify Excel general options.

   a. On the **File** tab, select **Options.**

   b. In the **Excel Options** dialog box, in the left pane, verify that the **General** tab is selected.

   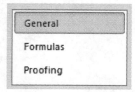

   c. In the right pane, in the **General options for working with Excel** section, from the **Color scheme** drop-down list, select **Blue.**

   d. In the **When creating new workbooks** section, in the **Include this many sheets** spin box, triple-click and type **5** to include five sheets by default in any new work-book.

   e. In the **Personalize your copy of Microsoft Office** section, enter your initials in the **User Name** text box and click **OK.**

   f. Save the file as *My Settings*

   g. Select the **File** tab.

   h. In the right pane, in the **Related people** section, observe that the user name entered by you prior to saving the file is displayed next to **Last Modified By.**

2. Explore Ribbon display options.

   a. Click the **Home** tab to view **Sheet 1.**

   b. Double-click the **Home** tab to hide the Ribbon.

   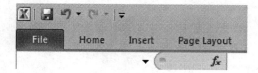

c. Observe that the tabs on the Ribbon are visible, not the groups. Click a tab to display its groups.

d. Press **Esc** to hide the groups again.

e. Double-click any tab to restore the Ribbon.

f. Right-click the Ribbon and choose **Minimize the Ribbon** to keep the Ribbon minimized.

g. Click the **Home** tab and then click anywhere on the worksheet.

h. Observe that the Ribbon is minimized when any cell on the worksheet is selected.

i. Save and close the file.

TOPIC B
Customize Workbooks

In the previous topic, you customized the Excel work environment. You can also customize the appearance and functionality of individual workbooks in a variety of ways. In this topic, you will customize workbooks.

When using workbooks, you may discover elements that need to be customized. You may want to provide more information about the contents of a cell without cluttering up the page, to navigate quickly to other locations through hyperlinks, or to create watermarks. Customizing your workbook will allow you to provide all the information necessary in a stylish and efficient manner.

Comments

Definition:

A *comment* is text pertaining to the contents of a specific cell. It is displayed in a pop-up text box instead of a worksheet cell. When a cell contains a comment, a small red triangle is displayed at the top-right corner of the cell. Comments can be used in any cell, regardless of the type of data that a cell contains. Comments in a cell are hidden by default and are visible only when you hover the mouse pointer over the cell. To identify comments from different individuals, each comment will display the individual user's name as specified in the **General** category of the **Excel Options** dialog box.

Example:

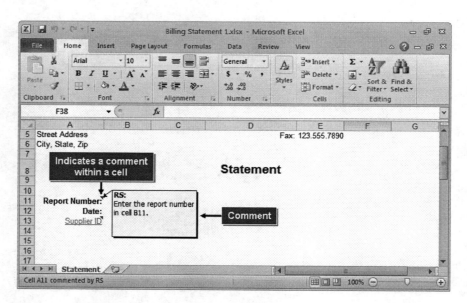

Figure 6-3: *Comments can be used for providing additional information.*

Hyperlinks

Definition:

A *Hyperlink* is a link that provides quick access to a location, called a *target,* where related information is available. The target may be a location in the same document, another file, a web page, or an email address. The hyperlink appears in the document as a picture or text. Clicking the hyperlink opens the target using its associated application.

Example:

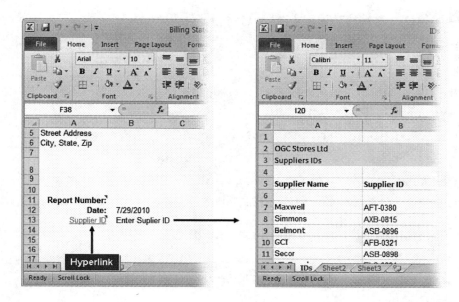

Figure 6-4: A hyperlink provides quick access to the related information.

Watermarks in Excel

A *watermark* is a text or graphical element that appears as a background on every page of a printed document. Watermarks help identify the status, urgency, or ownership of a document. They can include elements such as pictures, text, gradients, textures, or solid colors. In Excel, watermarks are implemented by inserting a graphic of an appropriate size in the header or footer area of the worksheet. The graphic is displayed behind text, starting from the top or bottom of every page, depending on where it is inserted. You can adjust the appearance of the picture so that it does not obscure worksheet data when printed.

Background Pictures

A *background picture* in a worksheet can be used for display purposes only, and it does not appear in printed documents. Each worksheet in a workbook can have a different picture in the background.

General Workbook Customization Options

Excel provides some general options that you can use to customize the look and feel of a workbook. These include:

- Hiding the gridlines.
- Hiding the row and column headings.
- Displaying workbook formulas rather than formula results.

How to Customize Workbooks

Procedure Reference: Add a Comment

To add a comment:

1. Select the cell to which you want to add a comment.
2. Add a new comment to the cell.
   - On the **Review** tab, in the **Comments** group, click **New Comment.**
   - Or, right-click the cell and choose **Insert Comment.**
3. In the **Comment** text box, type the comment text.
4. Click outside the **Comment** text box to add the comment.

Procedure Reference: Edit or Delete a Comment

To edit a comment:

1. Move the mouse pointer over the cell with the comment to be edited.
2. Enable the **Comment** text box for editing.
   - Select the cell, and then on the **Review** tab, in the **Comments** group, click **Edit Comment.**
   - Or, right-click the cell and choose **Edit Comment.**
3. In the **Comment** text box, make the necessary changes.
4. Click outside the **Comment** text box to complete editing the cell.
5. If necessary, delete a comment.
   - Select the cell, and then on the **Review** tab, in the **Comments** group, click **Delete.**
   - Or, right-click the cell and choose **Delete Comment.**

Procedure Reference: Insert a Hyperlink

To insert a hyperlink:

1. Select the cell in which you want to create the hyperlink.
2. Display the **Insert Hyperlink** dialog box.
   - On the **Ribbon**, on the **Insert** tab, in the **Links** group, click **Hyperlink.**
   - Or, right-click the cell and choose **Hyperlink.**
3. To create custom text for the hyperlink display, type the text in the **Text To Display** text box.
4. To create a custom ScreenTip for the hyperlink, click **ScreenTip**, type the text, and click **OK.**

5. In the **Link To** section, select the appropriate type of resource to link to.
   - **Existing File Or Web Page.**
   - **Place In This Document.**
   - **Create New Document.**
   - Or, **E-mail Address.**

6. Enter the target information for the hyperlink.
   - For a file, browse to select the file.
   - For a web page, select the address for the page from the **Address** drop-down list; or, type the address and click the **Browse The Web** button to locate the page.
   - For a location in the same document, type or select the cell or name reference.
   - For a new document, type the name of the document and select the path to create the new document. Select the appropriate option to edit the contents of the document now or later.
   - For an email address, type the address or select it from the list of recently used email addresses. If you want to include a default subject line every time you create an email by clicking the hyperlink, type it in the **Subject** text box.

7. Click **OK.**

8. Test the hyperlink by clicking it in the document. If the **Microsoft Office Excel Security Notice** message box is displayed, click **Yes** to close it.

Procedure Reference: Modify or Delete a Hyperlink

To modify or delete a hyperlink and its attributes:

1. Right-click the cell with the hyperlink and choose **Edit Hyperlink.**

2. In the **Edit Hyperlink** dialog box, make the necessary changes.
   - Modify the hyperlinked cell attributes.
     - To add a screentip to your hyperlink, click **ScreenTip** and in the **Set Hyperlink ScreenTip** dialog box, in the **ScreenTip text** text box, enter the text that you want to appear as the screentip. Click **OK.**
     - To add a bookmark to your hyperlink, click **Bookmark** and in the **Select Place in Document** dialog box, select the worksheet and specify the location of the cell that you want to navigate to in the hyperlinked document.
   - Modify the hyperlink.
     - In the **Text to display** text box, triple-click and type the desired text that you want to appear as a hyperlink.
     - In the **Link to** and **Look in** panes, specify the desired location of the file that you want to link.
     - In the **Address** text box, specify the URL of the web page that you want to view.

3. Click **OK** to save the changes.

4. If necessary, delete a hyperlink.
   - Right-click the cell with the hyperlink and choose **Remove Hyperlink.**
   - Or, select the cell with the hyperlink and press **Delete.**

Procedure Reference: Hide or Display Gridlines, Headings, and Formulas

To hide or display gridlines, headings, and formulas in a worksheet:

1. To display or hide gridlines, on the **Page Layout** tab, in the **Sheet Options** group, under **Gridlines**, check or uncheck the **View** check box.

2. To display or hide row and column headings, on the **Page Layout** tab, in the **Sheet Options** group, under **Headings**, check or uncheck the **View** check box.

3. Display or hide formulas rather than formula results.

   ● Hold **Ctrl** and press the **Grave Accent** key.

   ● Or, on the **Formulas** tab, in the **Formula Auditing** group, click **Show Formulas.**

 The Grave Accent (′) key is usually paired with the Tilde character (~) on the top row (or number row) of the keyboard. It is not on the function keys row.

Procedure Reference: Add a Background to a Worksheet

To add a background to a worksheet:

1. Select any cell in the worksheet.

2. On the **Page Layout** tab, in the **Page Setup** group, click **Background.**

3. Navigate to the folder containing the image to be applied as the background, select the image, and click **Insert.**

4. If necessary, to remove the background, on the **Page Layout** tab, in the **Page Setup** group, click **Delete Background.**

Formatting Pictures for Use as Watermarks

To create the effect of a watermark in Excel, simply insert the picture you want to use as the watermark in the header or footer of the worksheet. You will need to format the picture so that it appears properly behind the worksheet contents when you print the worksheet. If the picture is larger or smaller than the paper you will use to print, you should adjust its size. You should also adjust the settings for the picture so that it is lighter than the printed data. The **Washout** color setting is often a good choice. This increases the brightness but decreases the contrast. You might need to experiment with the settings so that the output appears properly on your particular printer.

ACTIVITY 6-2
Adding Comments and Hyperlinks to a Workbook

Data Files:

Billing Statement.xlsx, IDs.xlsx

Setup:

Right click the **Home** tab and uncheck **Minimize the Ribbon** to display the Ribbon.

Scenario:

As the store manager in OGC Stores, you have created an Excel file in which the invoice data can be entered. You decide to include comments in the Store Number and the Supplier ID cells, which can be helpful to the store employees entering the data. You also think that it would be helpful to add a hyperlink to allow quick reference to the Supplier ID numbers, which are in another Microsoft Excel file.

---

1. Add comments to cells A11 and A13.

    a.   From the C:\084577Data\Customizing and Enhancing Workbooks and the Excel Envi-
         ronment folder, open the Billing Statement.xlsx file.

    b.   On the **Statement** worksheet, right-click cell **A11** and choose **Insert Comment.**

    c.   In the **Comment** text box, type *Enter the report number in cell B11.*

    d.   Click anywhere on the worksheet to deselect cell **A11.**

    e.   The red triangle indicates that there is a comment in the cell. Place the mouse
         pointer over cell **A11** to view the comment.

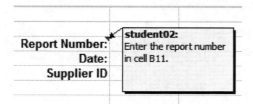

    f.   Right-click **A13** and choose **Insert Comment.**

    g.   In the comment box, type *The Supplier IDs can be found in an Excel sheet.*

    h.   Click anywhere on the worksheet to deselect cell **A13.**

---

2. Modify the comment in cell A13.

    a.   Right-click cell **A13** and choose **Edit Comment.**

    b.   In the **Comment** text box, change the comment to *The Supplier IDs can be found
         in an Excel sheet titled IDs.xlsx.*

    c.   Click anywhere on the worksheet to close the **Comment** box.

3.   Add a hyperlink to quickly look up the Customer ID in the IDs.xlsx file and verify its functioning.

    a.   Right-click cell **A13** and choose **Hyperlink.**

    b.   In the **Insert Hyperlink** dialog box, select **IDs.xlsx** and click **OK.**

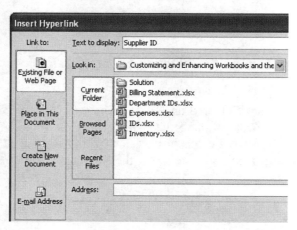

    c.   Click the **Supplier ID** hyperlink.

    d.   The **IDs.xlsx** file opens in a new window. Close the **IDs.xlsx** file.

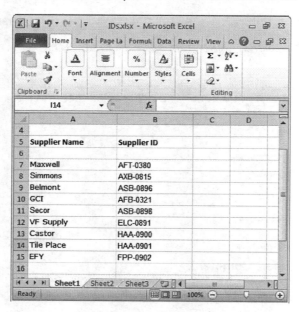

4.   Prepare the file for printing.

    a.   On the **Page Layout** tab, in the **Sheet Options** group, under **Gridlines**, uncheck the **View** check box.

    b.   Press **Ctrl** and then the **Grave Accent** key to display all formulas used in the worksheet.

The **Grave Accent** key (´) is above the **Tab** key on the left. It usually also has the Tilde (~) symbol on it.

c.   Press **Ctrl** and then the **Grave Accent** key to return to the values display.

d.   Save the file as ***My Billing Statement***

TOPIC C
Manage Themes

In the previous topic, you used an assortment of customizing options to modify various aspects of individual worksheets. A way to adjust the appearance of many workbook settings as a whole is to adjust the theme that is applied to the workbook. In this topic, you will manage themes.

Simply putting raw information into a spreadsheet doesn't mean that the application will be able to convey the intended message effectively on its own. A good visual representation of data is pleasing to the eyes and makes processing information a lot easier. By applying themes to your worksheet, you can enhance its look and feel.

Themes

Definition:

A *theme* is a unified set of formatting and appearance settings that can be applied to a workbook as a whole. Theme settings determine the fonts, colors, effects, and style sets that are available in a given worksheet, as well as the default appearance of workbook elements. Themes appear in the Themes gallery. There is always an active theme, but the default theme is Office. When you switch from one theme to another, Excel applies the appearance settings in the new theme to the corresponding elements in the workbook. There are many built-in themes; you can customize them or create new custom themes, and you can even download additional themes from the Office.com website.

Example:

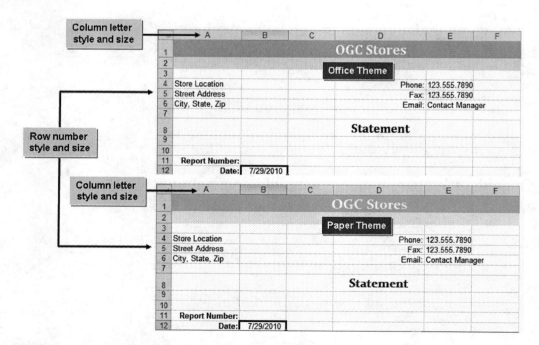

Figure 6-5: *The appearance of the Excel interface can be changed by changing the theme.*

Theme Modification Options

You can modify themes in a number of ways. You can either select different sets of colors, fonts, and effects to use in a theme, or create new colors and fonts to apply to different theme elements. If you modify the settings for a theme, you can save the changes either in the current theme or as a new custom theme. Once you save a theme, you can reuse it in any workbook.

Theme Colors Options

The **Theme Colors** section in the **Create New Theme Colors** dialog box contains options to set theme colors for different elements on your worksheet.

Option	Description
Text/Background	Displays color options to apply to the text and background.
Accent	Displays color options to apply to the different elements in your worksheet.
Hyperlink	Displays color options to apply to hyperlink text.
Followed Hyperlink	Displays color options to specify the color of the hyperlink after it is clicked.

How to Manage Themes

Procedure Reference: Create a New Theme Color

To create a new theme color:

1. On the **Page Layout** tab, in the **Themes** group, click **Colors** and select **Create New Theme Colors.**

2. In the **Create New Theme Colors** dialog box, in the **Name** text box, type a name for the color.

3. In the **Theme Colors** section, click the drop-down list for the element for which you need to apply a theme color: Text/Background elements, Accent elements, Hyperlink, or Followed Hyperlink.

4. From the **Theme Colors** gallery for the theme element, select a theme color or standard color to use for that theme color element, or click **More Colors** to select from the full color palette.

5. If necessary, set the other text/background colors and accent colors.

6. In the **Sample** box, verify the effect of the changes.

7. If you need to revise the color settings, in the **Create New Theme Colors** dialog box, click **Reset** to restore the default theme colors and then apply a new set of theme colors.

8. Click **Save** to save the new theme color.

Procedure Reference: Create a New Theme Font

To create a new theme font:

1. On the **Page Layout** tab, in the **Themes** group, click **Fonts** and select **Create New Theme Fonts.**

2. In the **Create New Theme Fonts** dialog box, in the **Name** text box, type a name for the font.

3. From the **Heading Font** and **Body Font** drop-down lists, select the desired font to apply for the headings and body text respectively.

4. In the **Sample** section, verify the effect of the font changes, and click **Save** to save the new theme font.

Procedure Reference: Create a Custom Theme

To create a custom theme:

1. If necessary, switch to the theme you want to use as the basis for the new theme.

    a. On the **Page Layout** tab, in the **Themes** group, click **Themes** drop-down.

    b. In the **Themes** gallery, in the **Built-In** section, select a theme.

2. In an open worksheet, use the **Colors**, **Fonts**, and **Effects** buttons in the **Themes** group to customize the current theme.

3. On the **Page Layout** tab, in the **Themes** group, click **Themes.**

4. In the **Themes** gallery, select **Save Current Theme.**

5. In the **Save Current Theme** dialog box, in the **File Name** text box, type a new name for the theme.

6. Click **Save** to save the customized theme. The theme will be saved in the **Document Themes** folder.

7. To apply the custom theme, select it from the **Custom** section in the **Themes** gallery.

ACTIVITY 6-3
Managing Themes

Data Files:

Inventory.xlsx

Before You Begin:

My Billing Statement.xlsx is open.

Scenario:

After creating a file for an invoice report, the store manager wants to ensure that the overall theme of the document matches the organization's color and font preferences. You have been asked to create a custom theme to be applied to all workbooks created by store employees for reporting purposes. After brainstorming with your colleagues, you decide to use "Angles" as the theme, "Foundry" as the color, and "Office Classic 2" as the font for the report.

---

1. Change the theme of the workbook to Angles and modify the theme.

    a. Observe the existing fonts, colors, fill colors and hyperlink color of the workbook.

    b. On the **Page Layout** tab, in the **Themes** group, click the **Themes** drop-down, and from the gallery, select **Angles**, which is the third option from the left in the first row.

    c. In the **Themes** group, click the **Colors** drop-down, and in the **Built-In** section, select **Foundry.**

    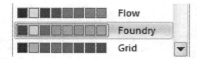

    d. In the **Themes** group, from the **Fonts** drop-down, select **Office Classic 2.**

---

2. Save the customized theme.

    a. Click the **Themes** drop-down and select **Save Current Theme.**

    b. Save the theme as *OGC*

c.   Click the **Themes** drop-down, observe that the saved theme appears in the **Custom** section, and then click the **Themes** drop-down to close the gallery.

d.   Save the file and close it.

3.   Test the custom theme by applying it to another workbook.

a.   From the C:\084577Data\Customizing and Enhancing Workbooks and the Excel Environment folder, open Inventory.xlsx.

b.   Observe the table and its current format on the **Inventory** worksheet.

c.   On the **Page Layout** tab, in the **Themes** group, click the **Themes** drop-down, and in the **Custom** section, select **OGC.**

d.   Examine the newly formatted table on the **Inventory** worksheet and save the file as *My Inventory* and close it.

TOPIC D

Create and Use Templates

So far in this course, you have manually formatted a workbook and modified or inserted many workbook elements. Once you have created a basic workbook structure, you might want to reuse the structure as a template so that you do not have to build an entire workbook from scratch. In this topic, you will create a workbook from a template as well as create your own customized workbook template.

Normally, when you begin a new workbook, you start with a blank worksheet. You have to enter data, create formulas, add formatting, and when it is just about done, there are changes. Implementing the same changes repeatedly would entail more work and wastage of time. Predefined and custom templates, however, provide formatted documents wherein all you need to do is to enter the data.

Templates

Definition:

A *template* is a worksheet that contains preconfigured formatting, formulas, and text. Some templates may contain standard data that can be used in combination with any other data that users may enter. The file extension for a template is .xltx. By default, templates are stored in the **Templates** folder. You can create multiple workbooks from a single template.

Example:

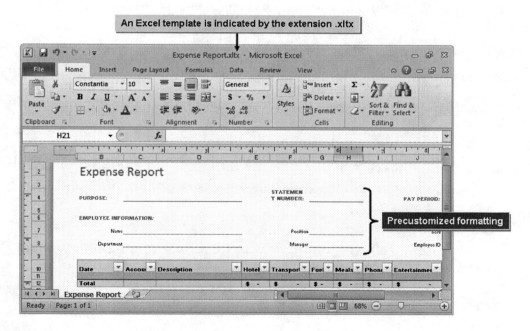

Figure 6-6: *An Excel workbook created from a predefined template.*

File Name for Workbooks Created from Templates

When a workbook is created from a template, the default file name of the workbook is the same as the file name of the template with a number added to it. In addition, the file extension changes from .xltx for a template to .xlsx, indicating that a workbook has been created from that template. For example, the default file name of a workbook created from the Billing Statement.xltx template will be Billing Statement.xlsx.

Types of Templates

Excel 2010 provides two types of templates: predefined and custom. Some predefined templates, known as available templates, are co-packaged and installed with Excel; for example, the Billing Statement and Expense Report. In addition to these available templates, you can also download predefined templates from Office.com.

Choosing Templates in Excel

You can select available templates from the **Available Templates** section of the window that appears when you click **New** in the **Backstage View.** You can also enter search text in the **Search Office.com for templates** text box to locate a particular type of template on Office.com.

How to Create and Use Templates

Procedure Reference: Create a Workbook from an Installed Template

To create a workbook from an installed Excel template:

1. On the **File** tab, select **New.**
2. In the **Available Templates** categories section, choose a category.
3. Open the required template.
   - In the right panel, select the required template and click **Create.**
   - Or, double-click the required template.

Procedure Reference: Create a Workbook from a Microsoft Office Online Template

To create a workbook from a Office.com template:

1. On the **File** tab, select **New.**
2. In the center pane, in the **Office.com Templates** section, select the desired template category.
3. The selected category might have subcategories. If so, click the subcategory.
4. If the template has a license agreement, read the agreement in the right pane and click **I Accept.**
5. The right pane will display a preview of the currently selected template and its details, such as download size and star rating. Download the required template.
   - Click **Download.**
   - Or, double-click the required template.
6. Click **Continue** to enable Microsoft validate your copy of Microsoft Office.
7. Excel will download the template and create a workbook based on it.

Saving and Reusing a Template

Once a template is downloaded and is not saved by default as a template, you have to download it again for using it. However, you can manually save it in your computer as an .xltx file. The saved template can be chosen from **My templates** or **Recent templates** category in the **Available Templates** section.

Procedure Reference: Create a Custom Template

To create a custom template:

1. Open or create the workbook you want to use as the basis for the template.
   - If you have a workbook file you want to base the new template on, open the workbook.
   - If you want to use the settings in an existing template as the basis for the new template, create a new workbook based on the existing template and make any workbook modifications that you need.
2. On the **File** tab, select **Save As.**
3. In the **Save As** dialog box, in the **File Name** text box, enter a name for the template.
4. From the **Save as type** drop-down list, select **Excel Template (*.xltx).**
5. The default save location will change to the **Templates** folder. To save it to another location, select the location from the **Save In** drop-down list and click **Save.**

Procedure Reference: Apply a Custom Template

To apply a custom template:

1. If necessary, create a custom template.
2. On the **File** tab, select **New.**
3. In the **Available Templates** section, select **My Templates.**
4. In the **New** dialog box, select your custom template and click **OK.** The new workbook will open with the same name with the number 1 at the end of the name.
5. Modify the new workbook as desired.
6. Save the file as an xlsx file.

ACTIVITY 6-4
Creating a Workbook from a Template

Before You Begin:

My Billing Statement.xlsx is open.

Scenario:

As the sales head for the eastern region, you keep receiving reports in different formats from different store managers in your region. To make data analysis easier, you want to standardize the report format and share it with all store managers in the region.

---

1. Enter the generic text that all store managers will need in the workbook and then save it as a template.

    a. From C:\084577Data\Customizing and Enhancing Workbooks and Excel Environment open My Billing Statement.xlsx.

    b. In cell **B13**, enter *Enter Supplier ID*

    > Supplier ID   Enter Suplier ID

    c. In cell **B4**, enter *Enter the Details in B4 to B6*

    > Enter the details in B4 to B6

    d. On the **File** tab, select **Save As.**

    e. In the **Save As** dialog box, from the **Save as type** drop-down list, select **Excel Template (*.xltx).**

    f. Verify that the template will be saved in the **Templates** folder, click **Save** and close the file.

---

2. Test the template by creating a worksheet from it.

    a. On the **File** tab, select **New.**

    b. In the center pane, from the **Available Templates** section, select **My templates.**

    c. In the **New** dialog box, verify that **My Billing Statement.xltx** is already selected and click **OK.**

d. Examine the title bar and verify that Excel has opened the file with the same name as the template and number 1 appended at the end.

> My Billing Statement.xltx1 - Microsoft Excel

e. On the **File** tab, select **Save As** to observe that the file extension is .xlsx.

f. Navigate to C:\084577Data\Customizing and Enhancing Workbooks and the Excel Environment.

g. Save the file as *My Billing Statement1* and then close the file.

h. Exit Excel.

Lesson 6 Follow-up

In this lesson, you enhanced workbooks using the features and tools available in Excel 2010, such as color schemes, comments, hyperlinks, and templates. These features and tools enable you to make your workbooks more functional and your work pattern more efficient.

1. **In which situations would you hide the Ribbon?**

2. **What are the various possible targets that might be included in your workbook hyperlinks?**

Follow-up

In this course, you used advanced formulas and functions and organized data in worksheets. You also used graphics to enhance your workbook and created PivotTables and PivotCharts for easy analysis and interpretation of data. Including these components in a workbook will help you to manage and streamline your tasks effectively.

1. **What are the uses and applications of functions in Excel?**

2. **What are the advantages of using charts while analyzing data?**

3. **Which features of Excel were most interesting to you?**

What's Next?

Microsoft® Office Excel® 2010: Level 3 is the next course in this series. In this course, you will learn a variety of techniques for collaborating with other Excel users, import and export data, and create macros to streamline workflow.

Lesson Labs

Lesson labs are provided as an additional learning resource for this course. The labs may or may not be performed as part of the classroom activities. Your instructor will consider setup issues, classroom timing issues, and instructional needs to determine which labs are appropriate for you to perform, and at what point during the class. If you do not perform the labs in class, your instructor can tell you if you can perform them independently as self-study, and if there are any special setup requirements.

Lesson 1 Lab 1

Calculating Test Score Data

Activity Time: 15 minutes

Data Files:

Test Scores.xlsx

Scenario:

You have been asked to present a report on the performance of students in different grades in different subjects. You decide to enter consolidation formulas for all individual sections and create a summary sheet.

For Each Section's Worksheet:

1. From the C:\084577Data\Calculating Data with Advanced Formulas folder, open the Test Scores.xlsx file.

2. Using the data given below, define range names for the entire workbook using the **Create from Selection** option.
   - Subject scores across grades (Math, Science, Language, Critical Reasoning)
   - Grade scores across subjects (Grades 7, 8, 9, 10, 11, 12)
   - The entire set of test data (B5:E10)

3. Using the range names, enter formulas that calculate the averages for each grade and subject.

4. For the performance information, enter a formula to evaluate against a benchmark of 77 percent. If the grade average is above, the word ABOVE should appear in the relevant cell; if not, the word BELOW should appear.

5. Create a formula using the range names to calculate the section average across all data.

For the Summary Sheet:

6. Enter the formula that will calculate the average 7th grade math score for all four sections.

7. Duplicate the formula for all grades and subjects on the summary sheet.

8. Enter the formula that will calculate whether the 7th grade average across all subject areas was above or below the benchmark of 77%. If the average is above or equal to the benchmark, the formula should return the label ABOVE. Otherwise, it will return the label BELOW.

9. Duplicate the formula for 8th through 12th grades.

10. Enter formulas to calculate the average scores for Math on the Summary sheet.

 You may notice that an average of 77.0% is displayed as ABOVE—this is because rounding off lies behind the spreadsheet and that the actual number may be higher.

11. Duplicate the formula for Science, Language, and Critical Reasoning.

12. Enter the formula that will calculate whether the performance in the subject is above or below average.

13. Save the file as *My Test Scores* and close it.

Lesson 2 Lab 1

Tabulating Data in a Worksheet

Activity Time: 15 minutes

Data Files:

European Sales.xlsx

Scenario:

As the sales head for the European region, you've collected raw sales data and are planning to present the sales trend in the region.

1. From the C:\084577Data\Organizing Worksheet and Table Data folder, open the European Sales.xlsx file.

2. Convert the data into a table.

3. Sort the data in descending order by the data in the **Total** column.

4. Add a Total row to the table.

5. Filter the Qtr1 data to show only those countries with greater than $5,000 in sales.

6. Save the file as *My European Sales* and close it.

Lesson 3 Lab 1
Representing Data Using Charts

Activity Time: 15 minutes

Data Files:

Math Quiz.xlsx

Scenario:

You want to use charts to represent the scores obtained by your students in a math quiz. There are many values in the data series, so you want to place the legend at the bottom of the chart, allowing the chart to be displayed in full width. You also want to add the title "Math Quiz Results" to the chart. To summarize the data, you decide to add the students' average to the worksheet and display this data on your chart.

1. From C:\084577Data\Presenting Data Using Charts folder, open the Math Quiz.xlsx file and create a 2-D column chart using the data in cells **A4:D22.**

2. Change the chart style to suit your preference.

3. Position the chart elements for the title and legends.

4. Enter the title as *Math Quiz Results*

5. Change the quiz labels in the worksheet as follows:
   - **B4:** *Factoring*
   - **C4:** *Least Common Multiple*
   - **D4:** *Greatest Common Factor*

6. Move the column chart to another worksheet titled *Math Quiz Result*

7. Save the file as **My Math Quiz.xlsx** and close it.

Lesson 4 Lab 1

Analyzing Data in a PivotTable

Activity Time: 15 minutes

Data Files:

Inventory.xlsx

Scenario:

Being incharge of managing the inventory of OGC Electronics, you need to present three reports with different outcomes in a meeting involving all board members of the company. Report 1 needs to display a list of all products, each store's inventory of that product, and a grand total by product and by store. Report 2 needs to display a list of all vendors, each store's inventory of that vendor's product, and a grand total by vendor and by store. Report 3 needs to display Rochester's inventory by vendor and the total cost of goods in inventory.

1. From the C:\084577Data\Analyzing Data Using PivotTables, Slicers, and PivotCharts folder, open the Inventory.xlsx file and create a PivotTable on a new worksheet using the data on the Inventory worksheet.

2. Create Report 1 by defining the row labels as **Product**, column labels as **Store**, and sum the units on hand.

3. Preview the report and save it as **My Inventory Report 1**

4. Create Report 2 by changing the row labels to **Vendor**

5. Preview the report and save it as **My Inventory Report 2**

6. Create Report 3 by filtering the column labels to display Rochester only; and then calculate the total sum of unit price.

7. Preview the report, save the file as **My Inventory Report 3** and close it.

Lesson 5 Lab 1
Inserting Graphic Objects

Activity Time: 15 minutes

Data Files:

OGC Bookstores Balance Sheet.xlsx

Scenario:

As the financial manager for OGC Bookstores, you have been working on the company's balance sheet. In your report, you want to draw attention to a couple of areas that need to be highlighted in the management meeting this week. The amount of cash available far exceeds the amount required for supporting current business needs, and it can be invested in other projects. Also, the Accounts Receivable amount is pending for a long time and efforts need to be made to collect on those accounts as soon as possible so that no dues are pending before the internal audit. Since the worksheet will be projected during the meeting, you want to make sure these areas stand out clearly. You will use text boxes and arrows to accomplish your goal.

1. From the C:\084577Data\Inserting Graphic Objects folder, open the OGC Bookstores Balance Sheet.xlsx file and insert a text box inside a rectangle shape for the cash amount. Indicate that the cash available far exceeds the current business needs and some amount can be used for other projects.

2. Format the shape using the **Intense Effect - Aqua, Accent5** shape style. Increase the weight of the text box outline to 1½ pt.

3. Insert an arrow that points from the text box to the cash amount.

4. Format the arrow shape and the text rectangle shape with the **Intense Effect – Aqua, Accent5** shape style. Change the font color of the text in the text box to **Black, Text 1** and bold format the text.

5. Insert a rectangle-shaped text box and arrow for the Accounts Receivable amount. Indicate that more effort should be made to collect outstanding dues.

6. Format the shape using the **Intense Effect – Aqua, Accent5** shape style. Change the font color of the text in the text box to **Black, Text 1** and bold format the text.

7. Save the file as *My OGC Bookstores Balance Sheet* and close it.

Lesson 6 Lab 1

Creating a Template with a Custom Theme

Activity Time: 15 minutes

Data Files:

Expenses.xlsx, Department IDs.xlsx

Scenario:

As the accounts manager of Our Global Company, you have received reimbursement claims relating to travel from the staff. You decide to apply changes to the list and use it as a standard template through which all employees can submit their travel expense claims.

1. From the C:\084577Data\Customizing and Enhancing Workbooks and the Excel Environment folder, open the Expenses.xlsx file and add the following comment to the Mileage reimb cell:

    The current reimbursement rate is $.60 per mile.

2. In cell **A21,** insert a hyperlink to the Department IDs.xlsx file so that users can look up their department IDs.

3. Create and apply a custom theme called ***My Company Theme*** with the following specifications:

    ●   **Median** theme
    ●   **Executive** color

4. Clear all details for the employee "Conner."

5. Save the file as a template titled ***My Expenses*** and close it.

Solutions

Activity 1-5

2. **True or False? The VLOOKUP function retrieves information from the columns that contain the value being searched.**

   __ True

   _✓_ False

Glossary

AND condition
A method for making database function queries more restrictive by including criteria in multiple columns on the same row within the criteria range.

ascending order
A sort order that displays data from lowest to highest value.

axes
The reference lines that are drawn on a graph for measuring the values. In charts displaying multiple data series, the X axis shows the data series in each category, and the Y axis shows how the data is measured (dollar amounts, time, and others).

background picture
A picture that is applied as background to a worksheet.

category (X) axis title
A chart item that describes what the X axis represents.

chart title
A chart item that describes what the overall chart represents.

chart
A visual representation of worksheet data that determines the relationship between different sections of the data.

clip art
A collection of predrawn graphic objects.

color scheme
A defined set of colors that is used to enhance the visual appeal of the application that you are working on.

comment
Text that pertains to the contents of a specific cell. Comments are displayed in a pop-up text box rather than a cell in the worksheet.

criteria
Within a database function, the range of data that contains field names and other data to match against the database field.

Cube function
A function used to fetch data from Online Analytical Processing (OLAP) cubes.

data labels
A chart item that indicates the numeric value, the percentage, or the name of a single data point.

data series
An individual set of values represented in a chart.

data table
A chart item that displays the worksheet data the chart is based on in a table below the chart.

database function
A type of function that performs a calculation only on data the meets certain criteria.

database

Within a database function, the argument that specifies the worksheet data range or table on which to perform the function.

Date & Time function

A function that assigns a serial number to date and time data in order to use the data in a calculation.

descending order

A sort order that displays data from highest to lowest value.

Engineering function

A function that performs various types of engineering conversions and tests.

field

Within a database function, the column within the database that you want to match to the criteria.

filter

A method of viewing data that shows only the data that meets a criterion.

Financial function

A function that performs a common accounting and financial calculation. The calculations are primarily based on depreciation of assets, investments, and loans.

function syntax

The general form of the function that provides the structure for entering function arguments properly to return the desired results.

graphic object

A visual element that can be inserted into a worksheet.

gridline

A chart item that indicates increments of a value.

grouping

A method of connecting multiple graphic objects to form a single graphic object.

HLOOKUP

a lookup function that searches horizontally across a table's column headings to locate and retrieve the information from the column.

hyperlink

A link within a document that provides quick access to related information, called the hyperlink target.

Information function

A function that performs analysis on a range of data to determine the type of data or formatting present in a cell.

layering

A method of displaying graphic objects that overlap other graphic objects in a specific order.

legend

A chart item that indicates what color or pattern used in the chart represents which particular data series.

Math & Trig function

A function that performs common trigonometric calculations such as cosine or tangent, or other specialized mathematical functions.

OR condition

A method for making database function queries less restrictive by including criteria in multiple rows within the criteria range.

PivotChart

An interactive chart that graphically represents the data in a PivotTable report.

PivotTable

An interactive worksheet table used to quickly summarize, organize, analyze, and compare large amounts of data.

PowerPivot

An Excel 2010 add-in that allows users to import data from various sources and analyze the data using PivotTables.

Quick Style set

A group of predefined formatting styles that have been selected to work together and reflect the theme of a worksheet.

range name

A method of referencing a range of cells using a name.

shapes

Simple geometric objects that are pre-created by Excel and can be modified and used to enhance your worksheets.

Slicer

A filtering tool that enables you to slice data and include only the elements you want in PivotTables and PivotCharts.

SmartArt graphic

A custom-made visual representation of the relationships between data, events, or ideas.

SmartArt

A collection of predrawn shapes.

sort

A method of arranging the data into a specific order.

Statistical function

A function that performs statistical analysis on a range of data in a worksheet or in a chart.

style

A named collection of formatting options that you can apply as a group.

subtotal

A function performed on a subset of data that has been sorted.

table

A section of contiguous rows and columns within a worksheet that Excel treats as an independent data set.

target

The information that a hyperlink points to.

template

A worksheet that contains preconfigured formatting, formulas, and text.

Text function

A formula that you can use to change the appearance of text in a worksheet by using the UPPER, LOWER, or PROPER function.

theme

A unified set of formatting and appearance settings that can be applied to a workbook as a whole.

three-dimensional (3-D) reference

A cell reference that is in the same location on each worksheet. A 3-D reference can be used only in a workbook with multiple worksheets.

value (Y) axis title

A chart item that describes what the Y axis represents.

VLOOKUP

A lookup function that searches vertically across a range's row headings and retrieves the information from the row that contains the value being searched.

watermark

A graphical element that appears as a background in a printed document.

Index

S

Screen capping tool, 111

shapes, 117

Slicer, 96

SmartArt, 110

SmartArt graphics, 124

sort

  ascending order, 48

  descending order

styles, 34

subtotals, 56

T

tables, 32

formatting, 42

  summary functions, 54

targets, 145

themes, 152

three-dimensional (3-D) cell reference, 9

V

value (Y) axis title, 71

VLOOKUP and HLOOKUP functions, 22

W

watermarks, 145